Go Programming
for Beginners

An Introduction to Learn the Go
Programming Language with Tutorials
and Hands-On Examples

Table of Contents

1. Introduction

There are legendary programming languages such as *C* and *C++* which are used to build platform and architecture specific and native software applications where the emphasis is usually on performance; and then there are all purpose scripting languages such as *Ruby* and *Python* which can do just about anything ranging from simple desktop applications to complex cloud applications. While languages such as Python and Ruby are easy to learn, easy to code and offer a super wide range of functionalities and libraries as compared to C/C++, the performance is not as good as C/C++ (sorry Python fans, but it's true!) unless there is dedicated hardware support for accelerating the applications. This is because a script is usually executed by a special software called as an interpreter which executes a script line by line where as a program written in C/C++ is compiled to generate executable code which is native to a hardware platform and then the executable code is run. *Go programming language* combines the performance of languages such as C/C++ and the ease of use of languages like Python.

Go programming language also known as *golang* or simply *Go* is a multi-paradigm programming language designed by *Robert Griesemer, Rob Pike, and Ken Thompson* at *Google*. It is a statically typed, compiled programming language that supports programming paradigms such as *object oriented, functional, imperative and concurrent programming*.

The development of Go began at Google in 2007 and the first stable version was released in 2012 following a public

1

announcement in late 2009. The developers used C++, Assembly language and Go (self-hosted) to implement Go programming language. There are two major implementations of Go – *gccgo* which is the front end for *GCC compiler* and Google's Go compiler which targets operating systems such as Windows, Linux, macOS and other Unix/BSD-like operating such as DragonFly BSD, FreeBSD, NetBSD, etc.

2. Scope

With Go language, you can build desktop applications, web applications, web services and much more. Google's Go language compiler toolchain is available for Windows, macOS, Linux and other Unix-like operating systems. With that toolchain, you can build applications targeted for Windows/Unix-like operating systems-based desktops and servers, embedded platforms, WebAssembly, etc. At present, there is not a stable GUI development framework available for Go, most of them are made available using wrappers and are still under development. But this is under no circumstances a turn-off because Go can do a lot of things. Containerization tool *Docker* which is revolutionizing cloud computing and virtualization space is entirely written in Go.

It is possible to access databases such as *MySQL, PostgreSQL, SQLite, etc.* with Go. You can even develop applications targeting some of the relatively newer technologies such as blockchain, data science, machine learning, etc.

One of the key selling points of Go is that it can build *WebAssembly* applications. *WebAssembly* is a type of code that can be run inside supported browsers. It is an open standard for executable binary code format targeted at web applications. This enables near native performance. With this feature, you can build a high performance web application written in Go language. With so much flexibility and such a wide use case scenario, Go is quickly becoming one of the most enterprise friendly languages with companies such as *Uber, Twitch, Google, Dailymotion, etc.*

making use of it to implement some of their applications and services.

Is prior programming knowledge needed to learn Go Programming language?

The short answer to that question is *No*. The long answer is – any prior programming experience will definitely help. Go combines the efficiency of languages like C/C++ and ease of use and code readability of languages such as Python or Javascript. If you know any of these languages, you will be able to relate to the concepts really well. But even if you are a complete beginner to programming or this is the first language you are learning, you should be able to learn Go with the right kind of mind set appropriate efforts. Having said that, you should be comfortable with using your computer. That is, you should know the way around your system, be comfortable with installing/removing software, using *Command Prompt, PowerShell, Terminal, Shell, etc.*

Who is this book for? What will I learn?

This book is for anybody who wants to learn the basics of Go programming language. The content has been carefully designed to suit complete beginners as well as experienced programmers. You will learn to build and execute simple console applications for desktops.

3. Getting Started

A PC with Windows/Linux or a MAC machine will be required to build Go applications. Go programs are plain text files (carrying the extension *".go"*) and hence you will need a text editor to write Go programs. Any text editor will do the job including *Notepad, Wordpad, vi, emacs, Notepad++, etc*. Chose an editor that you are the most comfortable with. You can alternatively use IDEs such as *Eclipse, IntelliJ, etc*. I prefer keeping it simple for learning basics, sticking to a simple text editor instead of an IDE. You will need to install Go compiler toolchain on your machine in order to build Go applications.

3.1 Install Go on Windows

Visit https://golang.org/dl/ and download the latest installer file for Windows having the extension *".msi"*. Once you have the file, execute it by double-clicking on it. You will need administrative rights to proceed. You will see a welcome screen as follows:

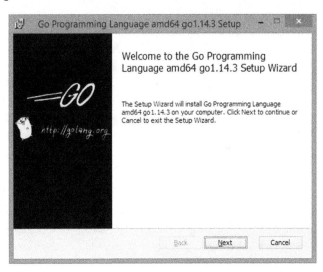

Click *Next* and you will be presented with the *EULA.*

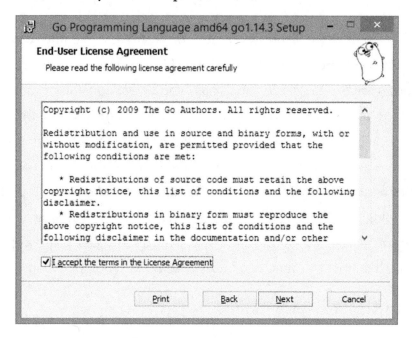

Read the agreement, accept the terms and click *Next.*

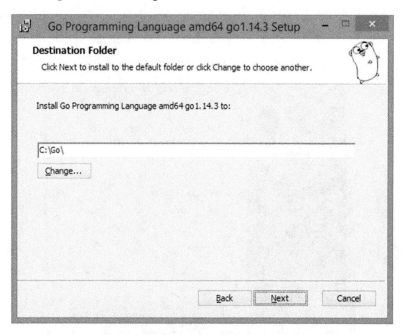

Here, you will be given an option to change the installation directory. It is best to leave it as it is and click *Next*.

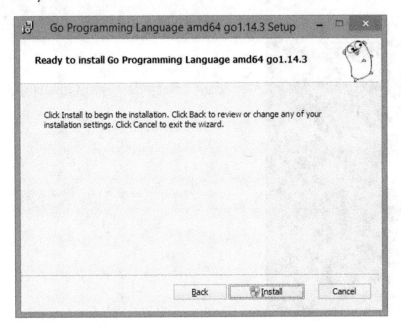

Click *Install* and the installation process will begin.

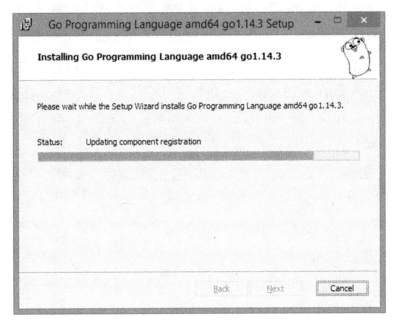

This may take a few minutes to complete. Once done, you will see something like this:

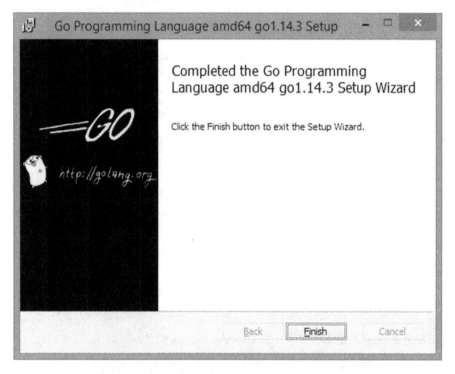

Click *Finish*.

Verify the Go installation by going to the **bin** folder inside the *Go installation directory* (usually *C:\Go* if you did not change it during installation) and make sure that an executable file called **go.exe** is present:

You can alternatively navigate to the Go installation directory using the command prompt with the help of *cd* command and list the contents of the directory using the *dir* command:

```
C:\Windows\system32\cmd.exe                               -  □  ×

C:\Go\bin>dir
 Volume in drive C is Windows
 Volume Serial Number is

 Directory of C:\Go\bin

27-05-2020  20:36    <DIR>          .
27-05-2020  20:36    <DIR>          ..
14-05-2020  19:29        15,004,160 go.exe    <===
14-05-2020  19:28         3,726,336 gofmt.exe
               2 File(s)     18,730,496 bytes
               2 Dir(s)  166,483,677,184 bytes free

C:\Go\bin>_
```

The Go installer automatically adds path of this *bin* directory to the *PATH* environment variable. This makes *go.exe* accessible from anywhere. To check, open **Command Prompt** or **PowerShell** and type the following command:

go

#OR

go.exe

If you see something like the following screenshot, it means that Go installation is successful and PATH variable is correctly set:

```
C:\Windows\system32\cmd.exe                                    _ □ ×

F:\>go
Go is a tool for managing Go source code.

Usage:

        go <command> [arguments]

The commands are:

        bug         start a bug report
        build       compile packages and dependencies
        clean       remove object files and cached files
        doc         show documentation for package or symbol
        env         print Go environment information
        fix         update packages to use new APIs
        fmt         gofmt (reformat) package sources
        generate    generate Go files by processing source
        get         add dependencies to current module and install them
        install     compile and install packages and dependencies
        list        list packages or modules
        mod         module maintenance
        run         compile and run Go program
        test        test packages
        tool        run specified go tool
        version     print Go version
        vet         report likely mistakes in packages

Use "go help <command>" for more information about a command.

Additional help topics:

        buildmode      build modes
        c              calling between Go and C
        cache          build and test caching
        environment    environment variables
        filetype       file types
        go.mod         the go.mod file
        gopath         GOPATH environment variable
        gopath-get     legacy GOPATH go get
        goproxy        module proxy protocol
        importpath     import path syntax
        modules        modules, module versions, and more
        module-get     module-aware go get
        module-auth    module authentication using go.sum
        module-private module configuration for non-public modules
        packages       package lists and patterns
        testflag       testing flags
        testfunc       testing functions

Use "go help <topic>" for more information about that topic.
```

If you see something like this – *'go' is not recognized as an internal or external command, operable program or batch file.* It either means there is a problem with the installation or the *PATH* variable has not been set correctly. In such a case, check the *PATH* variable using the *echo %PATH%* command, if Go's bin directory has not been added to it, add it manually through *System Properties* (*Windows Key + Pause Break*). If the *PATH* variable is correctly set and go command can still not be found, then go through the installation process once again.

3.2 Install Go on Unix-like Operating Systems

If you use a Unix-like operating system such as Linux, macOS, FreeBSD, DragonFly BSD, etc., download the appropriate installation file for your OS from https://golang.org/dl/. Installation process will vary from OS to OS. It is best to follow official Go documentation available at this link https://golang.org/doc/install in order to learn how to install Go on a particular OS.

Note: Programs demonstrated in this book have been written, built and executed on a Windows machine. They should compile off the shelf on Unix-like operating systems unless specified otherwise.

3.3 Compile and Execute Go Programs

As mentioned earlier, Go programs are plaintext files carrying the extension ". go". Go is a compiled language. That is, a special software called compiler converts a plaintext Go program in to an executable file. Here is a conceptual block diagram of the compilation process:

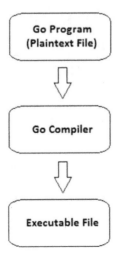

In simple terms, a Go program is given to a Go compiler which then converts the plaintext file to an executable binary file. Of course, there is more to this; there are many technical concepts involved in the compilation process but it is transparent to the user and hence there no need to learn about it unless you are into low level system software design or compiler design domains.

Let us now take a look at how to compile and execute Go programs.

3.3.1 On Windows

Open Command Prompt/PowerShell on Windows, navigate to the directory which has the program you want to compile and execute and enter the following command:

go build <program file>
Example:
go build test.go

When you enter **go build <program file>**, the **go** command refers to the **go.exe** file which is the Go compiler. The program to be compiled is passed as a command line argument to this utility marked by **<program file>** in the above command. If the compilation process is completed successfully, an executable file will be generated having the same name as that of the program file but with **".exe"** extension. For example, **go build test.go** command will generate **test.exe** file if compilation succeeds. If you want a custom output file name, you can use the –o flag as follows:

go build -o <output file> <program file>
Example:
go build -o xyz test.go

Once you have the output file, it can be executed as follows inside Command Prompt/PowerShell:

<executable file name>

Example:

test.exe

3.3.2 On Unix-like operating systems

Open Bash/Shell/Terminal on Linux, macOS or any other Unix-like OS, navigate to the directory where the program to be compiled is present and enter the following command:

go build <program file>

Example:

go test.go

When you say ***go build <program file>***, the ***go*** command refers to the Go compiler's executable file ***go*** usually present at ***/usr/local/go/bin*** directory. The program to be compiled is passed as a command line argument to this utility marked by ***<program file>*** in the above command. If the compilation process is completed successfully, an executable file with the same name as that of the program will be generated. This file will automatically acquire the execute permission. For example, ***go build test.go*** command will generate ***test*** file if compilation succeeds. If you want a custom output file name, you can use the –o flag as follows:

go build -o <output file> <program file>

Example:

go build -o test prog.go

The output file can be executed as follows within the terminal:

./ <executable file name>

Example:

./ test

3.3.3 Compile and Execute Demo

Let us get hands on experience to gain proper understating of how to compile a Go program and then execute it. The process will be demonstrated on Windows. If you use a Unix-like OS, follow *Section 3.3.2*.

On Windows, open your favourite text editor and copy-paste the following code:

```
package main

import "fmt"

func main() {
  fmt.Printf("\nIf you see this, you did a great job
so far!\n")

}
```

Save this file as ***test.go*** at a convenient location. This is your Go program to be compiled. A program can also be referred to as code, source, source code, source file or program file. Open Command Prompt or PowerShell, navigate to the directory where ***test.go*** is present using the cd command and enter the following command:

go build test.go

This command will generate a file called *test.exe*. Execute this file as follows:

test.exe

Here is the output:

Note: You do not have to understand what the above code does or how it works, the only purpose of this section was to teach you how to compile and execute a Go program.

3.3.4 Compilation Errors

Compilation errors occur when there are mistakes in the source file. These are usually syntax related issues. If you try to compile a Go program which has problems, the compiler will throw an error and the compilation process will not complete successfully and hence, the executable file will not be generated. Sometimes, the error message returned by the compiler will tell you exactly what has gone wrong where and sometimes it will not. Hence it is a good idea to check every program manually before compiling. Here is what a sample compilation error looks like:

```
F:\golang>go build test.go
# command-line-arguments
.\test.go:6:64: newline in string
.\test.go:6:64: syntax error: unexpected newline, expecting comma or )

F:\golang>
```

3.3.4 Go Playground

Go Playground is a web based tool used to compile and execute Go programs online. Of course, full functionality of Go will not be available through this tool but nonetheless, it is a very useful tool to try out small programs and learn concepts especially when you do not have access to a PC/Laptop with Go environment. Open your favourite web browser and visit https://play.golang.org/. You will see something like this:

```
package main

import (
        "fmt"
)

func main() {
        fmt.Println("Hello, playground")
}
```

Clear the existing code, copy-paste the code from *Section 3.3.3* and click *Run*. You should see the output right below the code area:

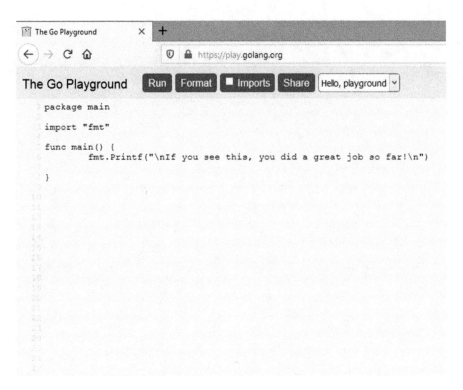

```
package main

import "fmt"

func main() {
        fmt.Printf("\nIf you see this, you did a great job so far!\n")

}
```

```
If you see this, you did a great job so far!

Program exited.
```

4. Syntax

Now that we know how to compile and execute a program, let us begin learning the actual programming concepts of Go language. Go is a case sensitive language. We may say that the words "programming", "Programming" and "PROGRAMMING" are the same but Go compiler treats all of them differently.

4.1 Statements

A statement is used to perform a task or a combination of tasks. It can be made up of anything such as operators, function calls, variable assignments, etc. In simple terms, a statement is a line of code that executes one or more instructions such as printing something on the screen, performing arithmetic operations, reading from a file, etc. In Go, one statement is placed on one line. Here are a few examples of statements:

```
fmt.Printf ("Hello")
var x int = 51
msg = "Go book"
```

4.2 Comments

Comments are used to mark or explain a piece of code. These are ignored by the compiler and have no outcome on the execution of a program. Hence, comments are only relevant to us humans. A comment begins with /* character sequence and ends with */ character sequence. Here are a few examples:

```
/*This is a comment*/
```

*/ * You can have any text within this character sequences */*

This book contains several programming examples. Each program contains comments which explain what a particular section of code does. Whenever you stumble upon programs in this book, make sure you read the comments well.

4.3 Identifiers

An identifier is a name given to a variable, class, object, function or anything else that is identifiable. Identifier names can contain alphanumeric characters but the first character has to be an alphabet. The only permitted special character is underscore (_).

4.4 Keywords

Keywords are reserved words that cannot be used as identifier names. Here is a list of keywords in Go:

break	default	func	interface	select
case	defer	Go	map	Struct
chan	else	Goto	package	Switch
const	fallthrough	if	range	Type
continue	for	import	return	Var

4.5 Tokens

A token is any meaningful item in a program. Keywords, identifiers, constants, symbols, string literals, etc. can all be called as tokens.

4.6 Basic Program Constituents

A very basic Go program should have the following constituents:

- **Package Declaration**

  - Go organizes source files inside the system as packages. A Go program can be used to build a library and also a standalone application. A standalone application is the one which executes on its own while a library cannot execute on its own, it has to be used in some other application. In this book, we will mostly be building standalone applications. The package name for standalone applications should be *"main"*. This tells the compiler that the Go program it is dealing with is supposed to be built as a standalone applications and not a library. This is how you would write a package statement:

    package <package name>
    Example:
       package main

- **Import Packages**

  - Packages are pre-built libraries which can perform various tasks. Go offers a rich set of packages for different things. Here is general syntax to import packages:

    import (
    <package 1>
    <package 2>
    <package 3>
    ...

...

<package n>

)

- For handling formatted I/O operations, *"fmt"* package is used. If you want to write a program to print something on the console, it is considered as a formatted output operation. You would be importing *"fmt"* package as follows:

import ("fmt")

- **Main Function**

  - A main function serves as an entry point of a program. A program will start executing from the first statement inside the main function. Here is how you would write a main function:

  func main () {

  *   /*Statements Here*/*

  }

Let us combine these program constituents and write a Go program that builds but does not do anything. It will have a package declaration statement and an empty main function. We will not be including *import "fmt"* statement because we are not going to perform any I/O operations:

```
/*Package Declaration Statement*/
package main
/*Mandatory main function*/
func main() {
}
```

Compile and Execute:

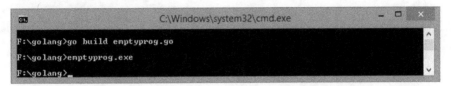

```
F:\golang>go build emptyprog.go
F:\golang>emptyprog.exe
F:\golang>
```

As seen, the program is built and run successfully. Nothing significant happens on the console as we are not doing anything inside the program. The program starts executing from the empty main function.

5. Hello World! Go Program

In the previous chapter, we saw what are the basic constituents of a standalone Go program. We also saw how to write a basic Go program that builds and executes but does not do anything. In this chapter, we will write a program to print something on the console. Printing something on the console is considered as an *Output operation*. We will be using a function called a *Printf* from the *fmt* package. It can be accessed as *fmt.Printf.* General syntax of using this function is:

fmt.Printf(<string>)

The *Printf* function should be given a string to print. A string is a sequence of characters. While giving a string to this function, the sequence of characters should be enclosed within double quotes. This function actually accepts a formatted string but for simplicity sake, let us only focus on a normal string and worry about formatted string later. If you want to print something on the console, the *fmt.Printf* statement will look something like:

fmt.Printf("Let us print something")

Let us combine whatever we have learnt and write a program to print *"Hello World!"* on the console:

```
/*Package Declaration Statement*/
package main
/*Import statement, import fmt package*/
import "fmt"
/*Mandatory main function*/
func main() {
 /*Print Hello World! using fmt.Printf function*/
 fmt.Printf("Hello World!")
}
```

Output:

Let us try the same program *in Go Playground*:

You can alternatively use the *Println* function from the same *fmt* package. This function inserts a new line at the end of the printed screen. General Syntax:

fmt.Println(<string>)

Example:

fmt.Println("Just another string…")

Here is the modified Hello World! program using **Println** function:

```
/*Package Declaration Statement*/
package main
/*Import statement, import fmt package*/
import "fmt"
/*Mandatory main function*/
func main() {
 /*Print Hello World! using fmt.Println function*/
 fmt.Println("Hello World!")
 }
```

Output:

As seen, there is an extra line of space left after printing Hello World.

If you want to insert a new line anywhere in the string, you can use the escape character sequence \n inside the string. This will work with **Printf** as well as **Println** functions. Here is an example:

```
/*Package Declaration Statement*/
package main
/*Import statement, import fmt package*/
import "fmt"
/*Mandatory main function*/
func main() {
 /*Print Hello World! using fmt.Printf function*/
 fmt.Printf("\nHello \nWorld!\n")
 }
```

Output:

```
C:\Windows\system32\cmd.exe                          –  □  ×

F:\golang>go build helloworld_2.go
F:\golang>helloworld_2.exe
Hello
World!
F:\golang>
```

There are many more escape character sequences. Another useful one is \t which will insert *one tab-space* in the output string. This will again work with *Printf* and *Println* functions. Here is an example:

```go
/*Package Declaration Statement*/
package main
/*Import statement, import fmt package*/
import "fmt"
/*Mandatory main function*/
func main() {
 /*Print Hello World! using fmt.Println function*/
 fmt.Println("\nHello\tWorld!")
 }
```

Output:

```
C:\Windows\system32\cmd.exe                          –  □  ×

F:\golang>go build helloworld_3.go
F:\golang>helloworld_3.exe
Hello    World!
F:\golang>
```

This is the chapter where we learned to build a meaningful console application which prints text on the screen. In almost every subsequent program, we will be printing something or the other on the console and hence you should know your way around *Printf* and *Println* functions really well. It is a good idea to play around with these functions and try to display different strings.

6. Data Types

A data type is used to categorize data. For example, a string is one type of data; a number is another type of data. Go offers 3 basic data types – **_Boolean, Numeric and Strings_**. Let us take a look at each one of these categories:

6.1 Boolean Data Type

A Boolean data type can only have two values – **_true_** and **_false_**. These are heavily used in decision making and control structures. This data type is referred to as **_bool_** programmatically.

6.2 Numeric Data Types

Numeric data types are used to deal with different kinds of numbers. This category can be divided further into 3 sub categories – **_Integers, Floats and Complex_**.

6.2.1 Integers

Integer data types as the name suggests are used to deal with integers. Go supports signed as well as unsigned integers of varying sizes. Here is a list:

Data Type	Description
int	Signed integer, size depends on the system (32-bit or 64-bit)
uint	Unsigned integer, size depends on the system (32-bit or 64-bit)
int8	8-bit signed integer
int16	16-bit signed integer
int32	32-bit signed integer
int64	64-bit signed integer
uint8	8-bit unsigned integer
uint16	16-bit unsigned integer
uint32	32-bit unsigned integer
uint64	64-bit unsigned integer
rune	Same as unit32. Used for Unicode characters.
byte	Same as int8. A byte is an 8-bit wide data.
uintptr	Unsigned integer used to store pointers to integers of all types.

Note: If you simply need a data type for integer, you should either use *int* or *uint*. The size will be decided depending on what kind of system you use. If you use a 32-bit system, the size will be 32-bits and for 64-bit systems, the size will be 64-bits. If you are specific with the size requirements of the data you are dealing with, you can use the data type of appropriate size.

6.2.2 Floats

This sub-category of numeric data types is used for floating point values.

Data Type	Description
float32	32-bit IEEE 754 floating-point number
float64	64-bit IEEE 754 floating-point number

6.2.3 Complex

Complex data types are used to deal with complex numbers having real and imaginary parts.

Data Type	Description
complex64	64-bit Complex Number having float32 (32-bit) type real and imaginary parts. Two 32-bit float32 types add up to 64-bits in total.
complex128	128-bit Complex Number having float64 (64-bit) type real and imaginary parts. Two 64-bit float64 types add up to 128-bits in total.

6.3 String Data Type

A string data type is used to deal with string values. A string is a sequence of characters. Programmatically, this data type is referred to as *string* in Go. We have already seen how to print a string using *Printf* and *Println* functions. More details will be covered in the next chapter.

6.4 Other Data Types

Apart from the 3 basic data types, Go offers some more data types which include – Aggregate data types and Reference data types. These categories of data types are covered in the relevant chapters of this book.

7. Variables

A variable is a uniquely identifiable name given to a memory location. When a variable is declared, some space is reserved for it in the memory depending on its type. For example, if you declare a variable of *int8* type, *1 byte (8-bits)* will be reserved in the memory; if you declare a variable of *float64 type*, *8 bytes (64-bits)* will be reserved for it in the memory. These memory locations have uniquely identifiable address which is usually in hexadecimal format. Because it would not be possible to work with memory addresses every time we want to access data we use variables. Naming rules for variables are the same as identifier naming rules – a variable name can contain alphanumeric characters; it cannot start with a number and the only allowed special character is *underscore (_)*. A variable can be declared using the *var* keyword with the following syntax:

var <variable 1>, <variable 2>, …. , <variable n> <data type>
Example:
/ *Declare 2 variables of type string*/
var first_name, last_name string
/ *Declare 1 variable of type int*/
var p int
/ *Declare 2 variables of type Boolean (bool)*/
var flag1, flag2 bool
/ *Declare 1 variable of type float32*/
var p float32

7.1 Variable Initialization

Variables when they are declared (using snippets shown above) will have *zero values*. That is, a Boolean variable will have a default *false* value, a numeric variable will have *0* value and a string variable will hold an *empty string* (*""*). You can set initial values to variables at the time of declaration. This process is known as *initialization*. Variables when initialized will hold the initial value that you set instead of a zero value. Here is the general syntax:

var <variable 1>, ... ,<variable n> <data type (optional)> = <value 1>, ... ,<value n>

Example:

/*Declare 1 int variable with value 1290, mention the type*/

var x int = 1290

/*Declare 2 float32 variables with values -36.58 and 59.37, mention the type*/

var a, b float32 = -36.58, 59.37

It is also possible to declare and initialize variables with mixed data types as follows:

var <variable 1>, <variable 2>, ... <variable n> = <value 1>, <value 2>, ... <value n>

Example:

/*Declare and initialize two Boolean values without mentioning the type*/

var b1, b2 = false, true

/*Declare and initialize 4 variables of mixed type*/

var name, age, height, is_working = "Adam", 19, 1.78, false

7.2 Short Variable Declaration

Short variable declaration is used to declare and initialize variables with the help of short declaration operator (:=). Using this method, you can skip using the *var* keyword however, initial value has to be assigned. General Syntax:

<variable 1>, <variable 2>, ... <variable n> := <value 1>, <value 2>, ... <value n>

Example:

/*Short declare and initialize an integer value*/

num := 31

/*Short declare and initialize variables of different types*/

msg, x, flag, y := "Hello", -6, true, 8.122

Note: Short declaration will only work inside a function. Variables declared outside functions will have to be declared with the *var* keyword. We will mostly be declaring variables inside functions unless specified otherwise. This concept will be clearer in the *Functions* chapter.

7.3 Variable Assignment

Variables can be assigned values using the de-facto assignment operator given by the *equal-to sign (=)*. For variable assignment to work, the variables must be declared first – either using the *var* keyword or using *short declaration*. If you try to assign a value to a variable that is not previously declared, the compiler will return an error. General Syntax:

/*Assuming the variables have been defined*/

<var 1>, <var 2>, ... <var n> = <value 1>, <value 2>, ...
<value n>

Example:

var x int

v = 20

var a float64

var name string

count := 0

a = -365.58901

name, count = "Max", 99

7.4 Printing Variables

The contents of a variable can be printed on the console using the **Println** function from the **fmt** package. Here is the general syntax:

fmt.Println(<var 1>, <var 2>, ... <var n>)

Example:

fmt.Println(name)

fmt.Println(a, b, c, d)

You can even use constant strings inside the **Println** function to label variables. For example:

var person_name, person_age = "Sasha", 23

fmt.Println("Name:", person_name, "Age:", person_age)

Note: While **Println** function does an alright job printing contents of variables, it is a crude method. The proper way to do this to use formatted strings with *Printf* function. This will be covered in the next chapter.

Here is a Go program that demonstrates the usage of variables:

```go
/*Variables Demo*/

/*Package Declaration*/
package main

/*Import Statement - import fmt package*/
import ("fmt")

/*Mandatory main function*/
func main () {
/*Declare 2 variables of type int using var
keyword*/
    var num1, num2 int
    /*Assign values to num1 and num2*/
    num1 = 10
    num2 = 20
    /*Declare and initialize 2 float32 variables using
var keyword*/
    var x, y float32 = -67.81, 45.76
    /*Declare and assign variables of mixed type using
var keyword*/
    var a, b, msg, flag = -5, 9.4, "Some text...",
false
    /*Short declare a complex number*/
    c1 := 2 + 3i
    /*Short declare variables of different data types*/
    p, q, country, c2, done := 178, -358.97,
"Argentina", 5 - 12i, true
    /*Print Everything*/
    fmt.Println("\nnum1:", num1, ", num2:", num2)
    fmt.Println("\nx:", x, ", y:", y)
    fmt.Println("\na:", a, ", b:", b, ", msg:", msg, ",
flag:", flag)
    fmt.Println("\nc1:", c1)
    fmt.Println("\np:", p, ", q:", q, ", country:",
country, ", c2:", c2, ", done:", done)
    }
```

Output:

```
Command Prompt                                    _ □ x

F:\golang>go build variablesdemo.go
F:\golang>variablesdemo.exe
num1: 10 , num2: 20
x: -67.81 , y: 45.76
a: -5 , b: 9.4 , msg: Some text... , flag: false
c1: (2+3i)
p: 178 , q: -358.97 , country: Argentina , c2: (5-12i) , done: true
F:\golang>
```

Note:

1. It is always a good idea to use meaningful variable names. For example, if you want to store the name of a person, you are better off naming that variable as *name* as opposed to something random such as *xyz*.

2. Declare the variables only if you need them. If you declare a variable and do not use it anywhere in your program, the compiler will give you a *"declared but not used"* error. This will prevent the program from building. If you somehow happen to declare the variable and not use it and want to avoid this error, you can assign the unused variables to the blank identifier given by the underscore sign *(_)*.

8. Output Formatting

In the previous section, we learned to use *Println* function to print variables. This function automatically leaves one line at the end, leaves a space between items when multiple items are printed. There is not much control although it does a good enough job if your objective is to simply print variables. For proper output formatting, we can use *Printf* function from the *fmt* package. This gives a much better control over the output; you will see why in a while.

The *Printf* function accepts a formatted string as an argument. A formatted string is made up of string literals and format specifiers called **verbs**. A verb is a character sequence which starts with a **percentage (%) symbol**. Different verbs are used for different data types. For example, for strings **%s** is used, for integers **%d** is used, etc. If a formatted string is given to a *Printf* function, variables, constants or expressions must also be given as arguments following the formatted string. At the time of printing, **verbs** will be substituted by the corresponding variables, constants or values resulting from the evaluation of a given expression. General syntax:

fmt.Printf (<formatted string>, <variables/constants/expressions>)
Example:
fmt.Printf ("Name: %s, Number: %d", name, num)

In the above example, first verb **%s** will be substituted by the value of **name** and second verb **%d** will be substituted by the value of **num** in the output. The following illustration will make things clearer.

fmt.Printf ("Name: %s, Number: %d", name, num)

Consider the following program:

```go
package main

import "fmt"

func main() {
/*Initialize string variables*/
    var first_name, last_name, city string =
"Samantha", "Hudson", "Denver"
    /*Initialize integer variable*/
    var age int = 33
    fmt.Printf("\nFirst Name: %s \nLast Name: %s \nAge:
%d \nCity: %s \n", first_name, last_name, age, city)
    }
```

Output:

```
F:\golang>go build basicverbdemo.go

F:\golang>basicverbdemo.exe

First Name: Samantha
Last Name: Hudson
Age: 33
City: Denver

F:\golang>_
```

Go offers many verbs, here are a few important ones:

Verb	Description
%v	Value in default format
%T	Data type of the value
%t	Boolean values – true or false
%d	Integers
%b	Binary (Base 2)
%o	Octal (Base 8)
%O	Octal (Base 8) with *0o* prefix
%x	Hexadecimal (Base 16) with (a-f) in lower case
%X	Hexadecimal (Base 16) with (A-F) in upper case
%c	Character
%f	Floating point value with no exponent
%F	Same as %f
%e	Scientific notation – floating point with exponent. *e* will be in lower case
%E	Scientific notation – floating point with exponent. *E* will be in lower case
%s	String
%p	Pointer

Here is a Go program that makes use of different verbs for different data types:

```go
package main

import "fmt"

func main() {
/*Declare and initialize a few variables*/
var x, y, z = 75, -6.872, 3+2i
var flag = true
msg := "Go Programming"
/*Print various things using Printf*/
fmt.Printf("\nx = %v Type: %T", x, x)
fmt.Printf("\nx (decimal): %d\nx (binary): %b\nx
(octal): %O\nx (hexadecimal): %X", x, x, x, x)
fmt.Printf("\ny = %f Type: %T \nz = %f Type: %T",
y, y, z, z)
fmt.Printf("\nflag = %t Type: %T", flag, flag)
fmt.Printf("\nmsg = %s Type: %T\n", msg, msg)
}
```

Output:

```
F:\golang>go build verbs.go

F:\golang>verbs.exe

x = 75 Type: int
x (decimal): 75
x (binary): 1001011
x (octal): 0o113
x (hexadecimal): 4B
y = -6.872000 Type: float64
z = (3.000000+2.000000i) Type: complex128
flag = true Type: bool
msg = Go Programming Type: string

F:\golang>
```

Note:

- The number of verbs inside a formatted string and the number of arguments following a formatted string should be the same.

- Always use the correct verb according to the data type of the value to be printed. When in doubt, use *%v.*

9. Operators

An operator is a symbol or a group of symbols used to perform one or more operations. Go offers arithmetic operators, relational operators, logical operators, bitwise operators and assignment operators. Let us take a look at each category of operators.

9.1 Arithmetic Operators

An arithmetic operator as the name suggests is used to perform arithmetic operations such as addition, subtractions, etc.

Operator	Description	Sample Usage	Explanation
+	Addition	x + y	Performs arithmetic addition, returns sum of the operands.
-	Subtraction	x - y	Subtracts operand on the right from the operand on the left and returns the difference.
*	Multiplication	x * y	Multiplies operands and returns the product.
/	Division	x / y	Performs division and returns the quotient.
%	Modulus	x % y	Performs division and returns the remainder. Operands needs to be of integer type.
++	Increment	x ++	Increments the value of the operand by 1.
--	Decrement	y --	Decrements the value of the operand by 1.

Note:

- When you divide an integer by another integer, the division operator will return an integer quotient even if it is supposed to be a floating point value mathematically. This is not a problem as such and is quite useful in some situation. However, if you want the floating point version of the quotient, you need to convert the operands to float first using *float32(<operand>)* or *float64(<operand>)*.

- In case of complex numbers, increment/decrement operators will only work on the real part.

- You can build a polynomial/expression using multiple variables and multiple operators. You can even use brackets to prioritize a particular operation.

Here is a Go program that demonstrates simple arithmetic operations on two integers:

```go
/*Arithmetic Operators Demo 1*/

/*Package Declaration*/
package main

/*Import Statement - import fmt package*/
import ("fmt")

/*Mandatory main function*/
func main () {
    /*Declare  6  variables  of  type  int  using  var
keyword*/
    var num1, num2, sum, diff, prod, mod int
    /*Declare float32 variable to store quotient*/
    var quo float32
    /*Assign values to num1 and num2*/
    num1 = 53
    num2 = 18
    /*Perform various arithmetic operations*/
    sum = num1 + num2
    diff = num1 - num2
    prod = num1 * num2
    /*num1 and num2 both are integers.
    Hence num1/num2 will result in an integer even if
the quotient is a float mathematically
```

```
    You need to convert both operands to float32 using
float32 (<operand>) before dividing. */
    quo = float32 (num1) / float32 (num2)
    mod = num1 % num2
    /*Print Everything*/
    fmt.Printf("\nnum1 = %d num2 = %d", num1, num2)
    fmt.Printf("\nnum1 + num2 = %d", sum)
    fmt.Printf("\nnum1 - num2 = %d", diff)
    fmt.Printf("\nnum1 * num2 = %d", prod)
    fmt.Printf("\nnum1 / num2 = %f", quo)
    fmt.Printf("\nnum1 (modulus) num2 = %d", mod)
    num1++
    num2++
    fmt.Printf("\nnum1++ = %d num2++ = %d\n", num1,
num2)
    }
```

Output:

Let us see how arithmetic operators work with floating point numbers. We have used the verbs *%f* for printing normal floating point values and *%E* for printing values in scientific notation format:

```
/*Arithmetic Operators Demo 2 - Floating point
arithmetic*/

/*Package Declaration*/
package main

/*Import Statement - import fmt package*/
import ("fmt")

/*Mandatory main function*/
```

```go
func main () {
   /*Declare 6 variables of type float32 using var
keyword*/
   var num1, num2, sum, diff, prod, quo float32
   /*Assign values to num1 and num2*/
   num1 = 0.0363257
   num2 = -2.93157E-3
   /*Perform various arithmetic operations*/
   sum = num1 + num2
   diff = num1 - num2
   prod = num1 * num2
   quo = num1 / num2
   /*Print Everything*/
   fmt.Printf("\nValues in normal floating point form
-> num1 = %f num2 = %f", num1, num2)
   fmt.Printf("\nValues in scientific notation form ->
num1 = %E num2 = %E", num1, num2)
   fmt.Printf("\nnum1 + num2 = %f", sum)
   fmt.Printf("\nnum1 - num2 = %f", diff)
   fmt.Printf("\nnum1 * num2 = %E", prod)
   fmt.Printf("\nnum1 / num2 = %E\n", quo)
   }
```

Output:

Arithmetic operators will also work on complex numbers. You can create complex number variables using the **complex64** or **complex128** data types. A **complex64** data type is made up of two **float32** data types, one each for real and imaginary parts and a **complex128** data type is made up of one **float64** data type for the real part and another **float64** data type for the imaginary part. The verb to be used is *%f* as a complex number is made up of two floating point numbers in Go. Alternatively, you can use *%v* too which will display a value using the original data type. A complex number variable can be initialized directly by specifying the real and imaginary part or by using a function called ***complex*** as follows:

<variable> := complex (<real part>, <imaginary part>)

Num := complex (1,8)

Here is a Go program that demonstrates the use of arithmetic operators on complex numbers:

```
/*Arithmetic Operators Demo 3 - Complex numbers'
arithmetic*/

/*Package Declaration*/
package main

/*Import Statement - import fmt package*/
import ("fmt")

/*Mandatory main function*/
func main () {
 /*Declare 6 variables of type complex64 using var
keyword*/
    var num1, num2, sum, diff, prod, quo complex64
    /*Assign values to num1 and num2*/
    num1 = 2 - 5i
    /*Use complex function to create a complex number,
does the same job*/
    num2 = complex (-3, 7)
    /*Perform various arithmetic operations*/
    sum = num1 + num2
    diff = num1 - num2
    prod = num1 * num2
    quo = num1 / num2
    /*Print Everything*/
    fmt.Printf("\nnum1 = %v num2 = %v", num1, num2)
    fmt.Printf("\nnum1 + num2 = %v", sum)
    fmt.Printf("\nnum1 - num2 = %v", diff)
    fmt.Printf("\nnum1 * num2 = %v", prod)
    fmt.Printf("\nnum1 / num2 = %f", quo)
```

```
/*Increment num1 and decrement num2*/
num1++
num2--
fmt.Printf("\nnum1++ = %v num2-- = %v\n", num1,
num2)
}
```

Output:

```
Command Prompt                                    - □ ×

F:\golang>go build complexarithmetic.go
F:\golang>complexarithmetic.exe
num1 = (2-5i) num2 = (-3+7i)
num1 + num2 = (-1+2i)
num1 - num2 = (5-12i)
num1 * num2 = (29+29i)
num1 / num2 = (-0.706897+0.017241i)
num1++ = (3-5i) num2-- = (-4+7i)

F:\golang>_
```

9.2 Relational Operators

Relational operators are used to compare operands. The result of the comparison can either be *Boolean (bool) true* or *false*. This category of operators is very useful when working with control structures.

Operator	Description	Sample Usage	Explanation
==	Equal To	x == y	Returns *true* if the values of the operands are *EQUAL, false* otherwise.
!=	Not Equal To	x != y	Returns *true* if the values of the operands are *NOT EQUAL, false* otherwise.
<	Less Than	x < y	Returns *true* if the value of the left operand is less than the value of the operand on the right, *false* otherwise.
>	Greater Than	x > y	Returns *true* if the value of the left operand is greater than the value of the operand on the right, *false* otherwise.

<=	Less Than OR Equal To	x <= y	Returns true if the value of the left operand is less than *OR* *EQUAL TO* the value of the operand on the right, *false* otherwise.
>=	Greater Than OR Equal To	x >= y	Returns *true* if the value of the left operand is greater than *OR* *EQUAL To* the value of the operand on the right, *false* otherwise.

Here is a program that demonstrates the usage of relational operators. The verb *%t* is used to display the Boolean result of comparison operations:

```
/*Relational Operators Demo*/

/*Package Declaration*/
package main

/*Import Statement - import fmt package*/
import ("fmt")

/*Mandatory main function*/
func main () {
/*Declare variables of type int using var keyword*/
var a, b, c, d int = -1, 3, -1, 9
/*Print a, b, c, d*/
fmt.Printf("\na = %d b = %d c = %d d = %d\n", a, b,
c, d)
/*Print result of comparison operations*/
fmt.Printf("\na == c: %t", a == c)
fmt.Printf("\nb == d: %t", b == d)
fmt.Printf("\na != c: %t", a != c)
fmt.Printf("\nb != d: %t", b != d)
fmt.Printf("\na < b: %t", a < b)
fmt.Printf("\nc > d: %t", c > d)
fmt.Printf("\nd <= b: %t", d <= b)
fmt.Printf("\na >= c d: %t\n", a >= c)
}
```

Output:

```
F:\golang>go build relationaloperators.go
F:\golang>relationaloperators.exe
a = -1 b = 3 c = -1 d = 9
a == c: true
b == d: false
a != c: false
b != d: true
a < b: true
c > d: false
d <= b: false
a >= c d: true
F:\golang>
```

9.3 Logical Operators

Logical operators are used to perform operations such as *Logical AND*, *Logical OR* and *Logical NOT* on Boolean operands. Variables holding Boolean values (*true* or *false*) as well as expressions (perhaps using *Relational Operators*) that result in *true* or *false* can be considered as operands.

Operator	Description	Sample Usage	Explanation
&&	Logical AND	(Expression 1) && (Expression 2)	Returns *true* if all the operands are *true*. Returns *false* if any one of the operands is *false*.
||	Logical OR	(Expression 1) && (Expression 2)	Returns *true* if any of the operands is *true*. Returns *false* if all of the operands are *false*.
!	Logical NOT	!(Expression 1)	Inverts the value of the operand. If the operand is *true*, *false* will be returned and if the operand is *false*, *true* will be returned.

Note: If expressions are used as operands, they will be evaluated first.

Here is a Go program that shows how logical operators work:

```go
/*Logical Operators Demo*/

/*Package Declaration*/
package main

/*Import Statement - import fmt package*/
import ("fmt")

/*Mandatory main function*/
func main () {
    /*Declare  variables  of  type  float32  using  var
keyword*/
    var a, b, c float32 = -65.736, 54.642, 0.003
    /*Short declare two boolean variables*/
    x := true
    y := false
    /*Print results of various operations*/
    fmt.Printf("\nx = %t y = %t", x, y)
    fmt.Printf("\nx || y = %t, x && y = %t, !x = %t, !y
= %t", x || y , x && y , !x , !y)
    fmt.Printf("\n(a < b) && (b > c) = %t", (a < b) &&
(b > c))
    fmt.Printf("\n(a == c) || (c != b) = %t", (a == c)
|| (c != b))
    fmt.Printf("\n(b != c) && (c <= a) = %t", (b != c)
&& (c <= a))
    fmt.Printf("\n(a == b) || x = %t\n", (a == b) || x)
    }
```

Output:

```
F:\golang>go build logicaloperators.go
F:\golang>logicaloperators.exe
x = true y = false
x || y = true, x && y = false, !x = false, !y = true
(a < b) && (b > c) = true
(a == c) || (c != b) = true
(b != c) && (c <= a) = false
(a == b) || x = true
F:\golang>
```

9.4 Bitwise Operators

Bitwise operators work on individual bits of operands. Operations will be carried out in a bit-by-bit manner. In order to understand this class of operators, you need to understand little bit of the binary number system and Boolean algebra.

Operator	Description	Sample Usage	Explanation
&	Bitwise Logical AND	x & y	Performs logical *AND* on each of the operands on a bit-by-bit basis.
|	Bitwise Logical OR	x | y	Performs logical *OR* on each of the operands on a bit-by-bit basis.
^	Bitwise Logical XOR	x ^ y	Performs logical *XOR* on each of the operands on a bit-by-bit basis.
<<	Left Shift	x << y	Bits of left operand will be left shifted by a number of times specified by the right operand. For example, *x << 3* will left shift *x's* bits *3 times*.
>>	Right Shift	x >> y	Bits of left operand will be right shifted by a number of times specified by the right operand. For example, *y >> 5* will right shift *y's* bits *5 times*.

Here is a demo on bitwise operators. The verbs *%b* and *%X* have been used to print values in binary and hexadecimal formats respectively.

9. Operators

```go
/*Bitwise Operators Demo*/

/*Package Declaration*/
package main

/*Import Statement - import fmt package*/
import ("fmt")

/*Mandatory main function*/
func main () {
/*Declare two integers*/
var x, y int = 23, 42
/*Print values of x and y in decimal, binary and
hex format*/
fmt.Printf("\nx (decimal) = %d, x (binary) = %b, x
(hexadecimal) = %X", x, x, x)
fmt.Printf("\ny (decimal) = %d, y (binary) = %b, y
(hexadecimal) = %X", y, y, y)
/*Print the result of bitwise operations*/
fmt.Printf("\n\nBitwise AND (&)\nx & y (decimal) =
%d, x & y (binary) = %b, x & y (hexadecimal) = %X\n", x
& y, x & y, x & y)
fmt.Printf("\nBitwise OR (|)\nx | y (decimal) = %d,
x | y (binary) = %b, x | y (hexadecimal) = %X\n", x |
y, x | y, x | y)
fmt.Printf("\nBitwise XOR (^)\nx ^ y (decimal) =
%d, x ^ y (binary) = %b, x ^ y (hexadecimal) = %X\n", x
^ y, x ^ y, x ^ y)
fmt.Printf("\nLeft Shift (<<)\nx << 1 (decimal) =
%d, x << 1 (binary) = %b, x << 1 (hexadecimal) = %X\n",
x << 1, x << 1, x << 1)
fmt.Printf("\nRight Shift (>>)\ny >> 3 (decimal) =
%d, y >> 3 (binary) = %b, y >> 3 (hexadecimal) = %X\n",
y >> 3, y >> 3, y >> 3)
}
```

Output:

9.5 Assignment Operators

We already know about the de-facto assignment operator given by the *equal-to sign (=)*. There are more operators in Go which perform compound assignment operations.

Operator	Description	Sample Usage	Equivalent To
+=	Perform arithmetic addition, then assign sum to the operand on the left.	x += y	x = x + y
-=	Subtract operand on the right from the operand on the left and assign difference to the operand on the left.	x -= y	x = x − y
*=	Multiply operands and assign product to the operand on the left.	x *= y	x = x * y
/=	Divide the operand on the left by the operand on the right and assign quotient to the operand on the left.	x /= y	x = x / y

%=	Divide the operand on the left by the operand on the right and assign remainder to the operand on the left.	x %= y	x = x % y
&=	Perform Bitwise Logical AND, assign result to the operand on the left.	x &= y	x = x & y
|=	Perform Bitwise Logical OR, assign result to the operand on the left.	x |= y	x = x | y
^=	Perform Bitwise Logical XOR, assign result to the operand on the left.	x ^= y	x = x ^ y
<<=	Perform left shift, assign result to the operand on the left.	x <<= y	x = x << y
>>=	Perform right shift, assign result to the operand on the left.	x >>= y	x = x >> y

Let us write a Go program to demonstrate the usage of different assignment operators.

```go
/*Assignment Operators Demo*/

/*Package Declaration*/
package main

/*Import Statement - import fmt package*/
import ("fmt")

/*Mandatory main function*/
func main () {
/*Declare two integers*/
var num1, num2 int = 35, 20
fmt.Printf("\nnum1 = %d num2 = %d", num1, num2)
/*Perform various compound assignment operations
and print*/
num1 += num2
fmt.Printf("\nnum1 += num2 = %d", num1)
num1 -= num2
fmt.Printf("\nnum1 -= num2 = %d", num1)
num1 *= num2
fmt.Printf("\nnum1 *= num2 = %d", num1)
```

```
    num1 /= num2
    fmt.Printf("\nnum1 /= num2 = %d", num1)
    num1 %= num2
    fmt.Printf("\nnum1 (mod)= num2 = %d", num1)
    num1 &= num2
    fmt.Printf("\nnum1  &=  num2  =  %d  (decimal)  /  %b
(binary)", num1, num1)
    num1 |= num2
    fmt.Printf("\nnum1  |=  num2  =  %d  (decimal)  /  %b
(binary)", num1, num1)
    num1 ^= num2
    fmt.Printf("\nnum1  ^=  num2  =  %d  (decimal)  /  %b
(binary)", num1, num1)
    num2 <<= 1
    fmt.Printf("\nnum2  <<=  1  =  %d  (decimal)  /  %b
(binary)", num2, num2)
    num2 >>= 3
    fmt.Printf("\nnum2  >>=  3  =  %d  (decimal)  /  %b
(binary)\n", num2, num2)
    }
```

Output:

```
F:\golang>go build assignmentoperators.go

F:\golang>assignmentoperators.exe

num1 = 35 num2 = 20
num1 += num2 = 55
num1 -= num2 = 35
num1 *= num2 = 700
num1 /= num2 = 35
num1 (mod)= num2 = 15
num1 &= num2 = 4 (decimal) / 100 (binary)
num1 |= num2 = 20 (decimal) / 10100 (binary)
num1 ^= num2 = 0 (decimal) / 0 (binary)
num2 <<= 1 = 40 (decimal) / 101000 (binary)
num2 >>= 3 = 5 (decimal) / 101 (binary)

F:\golang>
```

10. User Interaction

Up to this point, we have seen several programming examples. All those programs had hard coded values. None of the programs gave the user an opportunity to enter values manually. In this section, we will learn how to accept input from the user.

There are many ways to interact with the user. We will learn about two simple functions from the *fmt* package used for reading input from the user – *Scanln* and *Scanf.*

10.1 Scanln Function

Here is how to use the *Scanln* fucntion:

fmt.Scanln (&<string variable>)

Example:

var str string;

smt.Scanln (&str)

The *Scanln* function requires a string variable to be specified to store user's input marked by **<string variable>** in the above code snippet. This function implements a **blocking I/O operation**. That is, when the execution control will reach a *Scanln* statement, the execution of the program will halt to give the user an opportunity to enter something through the keyboard (and press Enter). Once the user enters something and hits Enter, whatever the user has entered through the keyboard will be fetched and stored in the specified string variable. The **ampersand sign (&)** before the variable is used to fetch the memory address of the variable so that the *Scanln* function can directly set the contents of the specified variable. This concept will be clearer in the *Pointers* chapters. Let us write a simple Go program to prompt the user to enter something and display it back:

```go
/*User Interaction Demo 1*/
/*Package Declaration*/
package main
/*Import Statement - import fmt package*/
import ("fmt")
/*Mandatory main function*/
func main () {
 /*Create a variable to store input*/
 var str string;
 /*Prompt the user to enter something*/
 fmt.Printf("\nEnter something: ")
 /*Read user input using Scanln function*/
 fmt.Scanln(&str)
 /*Display whatever has been read*/
 fmt.Printf("\nYou have entered: %s \n", str)
}
```

Output:

The *Scanln* function has its own limitations. To start with, it can only read the input in a string format. That means, even if you enter a number, it will be treated as a string. Second, it reads input as a space-separated tokenized string. That is, if you enter a sentence, each word will be treated as a token and those many variables will be needed to store the input. If you specify only one variable and enter a sentence, only the first word will be read. Let us run the same program and try to enter a sentence:

As seen, only the first word is read. The above input had four words and hence the *Scanln* statement should have had 4 variables specified to store those 4 words as follows:

fmt.Scanln(&str1, &str2, &str3, &str4)

Similarly, the Printf statement should look like:

fmt.Printf("\nYou have entered: %s %s %s %s\n ", str1, str2, str3, str4)

Here is the full program:

```
/*User Interaction Demo 2*/
/*Package Declaration*/
package main
/*Import Statement - import fmt package*/
import ("fmt")
/*Mandatory main function*/
func main () {
 /*Create variables to store input*/
 var str1, str2, str3, str4 string;
 /*Prompt the user to enter something*/
 fmt.Printf("\nEnter something: ")
 /*Read user input using Scanln function*/
 fmt.Scanln(&str1, &str2, &str3, &str4)
 /*Display whatever has been read*/
 fmt.Printf("\nYou have entered: %s %s %s %s\n ",
str1, str2, str3, str4)
 }
```

Output:

```
F:\golang>go build userinteraction_1.go
F:\golang>userinteraction_1.exe
Enter something: Here is a demo...
You have entered: Here is a demo...
F:\golang>_
```

Although the program works correctly now, this is not the best way to read a sentence as we do not know how big a sentence a user will enter. One variable will be required to store one word. This is not at all practical. There is a better way to read sentences using the **bufio** package discussed later in this chapter. We will use the **Scanln** function only when we want to read one word or one number at a time. If the user enters a number and you try to read it using **Scanln**, it will be in the string format. In order to convert a number in string format to the appropriate numeric format, we will use functions from the **strconv** package. The first thing you will have to do is import this package in your program and use the following conversion functions:

Convert a number in string format to integer:

<number variable>, <error variable> = strconv.Atoi(<number in string format>)

Example:

num, err := strconv.Atoi("55")

In the above example, **"55"** in string format will be converted to **55** in integer format and stored in the variable **num** which is short declared here. Along with that, **err** has also been short declared which will be used to store conversion error if any.

Convert a number in string format to float:

<variable> = *strconv.ParseFloat(<number in string format>, <number of bits>)*

Example:

numS := "-46.2343"

numF, err := strconv.ParseFloat(numS, 64)

In the above example, the **ParseFloat** function will convert **"-46.2343"** in string format to **-46.2343** in 64-bit float format and return it to the **numF** variable where it will be stored.

Let us write a Go program to accept 4 numbers from the user – two integers and two floats. We will use **Scanln** function to read these inputs and hence all 4 numbers will be stored in string format. We will convert these numbers to the appropriate formats and perform addition, subtraction, multiplication and division:

```
/*User Interaction Demo 3 - Work with numbers */
/*Package Declaration*/
package main
/*Import   Statement   -   import  fmt   and   strconv
package*/
    import (
        "fmt"
        "strconv"
        )
    /*Mandatory main function*/
    func main () {
    /*Declare variables to store input*/
    var num1_str, num2_str, num3_str, num4_str string
    /*Declare    variables    to    store    int    and
float64equivalents*/
    var num1, num2, sum, diff int
    var num3, num4, prod, quo float64
```

```
/*Prompt the user to enter two integers*/
fmt.Printf("\nEnter two inegers: ")
/*Read user input using Scanln function*/
fmt.Scanln(&num1_str, &num2_str)
/*Prompt the user to enter two floats*/
fmt.Printf("\nEnter two floats: ")
/*Read user input using Scanln function*/
fmt.Scanln(&num3_str, &num4_str)
/*Convert num1_str and num2_str to integer*/
num1, err1 := strconv.Atoi(num1_str)
num2, err2 := strconv.Atoi(num2_str)
/*Convert num3_str and num4_str to float64*/
num3, err3 := strconv.ParseFloat(num3_str, 64)
num4, err4 := strconv.ParseFloat(num4_str, 64)
/*Assign err to blank identifiers*/
_ = err1
_ = err2
_ = err3
_ = err4
/*Perform arithmetic operations*/
sum = num1 + num2
diff = num1 - num2
prod = num3 * num4
quo = num3 / num4
/*Print everything*/
fmt.Printf("\nnum1 + num2 = %d", sum)
fmt.Printf("\nnum1 - num2 = %d", diff)
fmt.Printf("\nnum3 * num4 = %f", prod)
fmt.Printf("\nnum3 / num4 = %f \n", quo)
}
```

Note: We have used 4 different error variables – *err1, err2, err3 and err4* for 4 different conversions. There is no need to use them. However, if you do not use them, the compiler will return a *"declared but not used"* error and the program will not build. To circumvent this problem, each of these error variables can be assigned to the *blank identifier _.*

Output:

10.2 Scanf Function

The **Scanf** function is quite similar to the one used in **C language**. This function uses **verbs** (analogous to **format specifiers** in C) to read data of particular types. For example, if you want to read an integer from the user, you can use the verb **%d**. This eliminates the extra step of data conversion used in **Scanln**. The same verbs discussed in **Chapter 8** will be used. Here is the general syntax:

fmt.Scanf("<formatted string with verbs>", &<variables separated by comma>)

fmt.Scanf("%<verb 1> %<verb 2>, ...", &<var 1>, &<var 2>, ...)

Example:

fmt.Scanf("%s %d %f", &name, &age, &weight)

The **Scanf** function uses a formatted string made up of verbs to parse user's input. For every verb used, there is a corresponding variable (where variable name is prefixed with an **ampersand sign**). This function also implements **blocking I/O operation**. When the user enters something through the keyboard, it will be parsed according to the format specified in the formatted string. For example, if the formatted string looks like this – *"%s %d %f"*, the user is suppose to enter three values separated by a space where the first value is a *string*, the second value is an *integer* and the third value is a *float*. Enter is suppose to be pressed only when all the values are entered. If the user presses enter after entering the first value, the remaining two inputs will be skipped and the corresponding variables will get zero-values. Let us take another example of a formatted string. If the formatted string looks like this – *"%d\n%f\n%d\n%s"*, the function will expect 4 inputs from the user. The *"\n"* character sequence between the verbs indicates that the user is suppose to press enter after entering each input. If this is getting confusing, you can always use one *Scanf* statement for one input. Let us write a program to read 3 inputs from a user and print whatever the user has entered back:

```
/*Scanf Demo*/
/*Package Declaration*/
package main
/*Import Statement - import fmt package*/
import ("fmt")
/*Mandatory main function*/
func main () {
 /*Declare Variables*/
 var name string
 var age int
 var weight float32
 /*Prompt the user to enter 3 values*/
 fmt.Printf("\nEnter name, age and weight: ")
 /*Read 3 values*/
 fmt.Scanf("%s %d %f", &name, &age, &weight)
 /*Display everything*/
```

```
fmt.Printf("\n\nName: %s, Age: %d, Weight: %f \n",
name, age, weight)
    }
```

Output:

```
C:\Windows\system32\cmd.exe

F:\golang>go build scanfdemo.go
F:\golang>scanfdemo.exe
Enter name, age and weight: Liev 18 152

Name: Liev, Age: 18, Weight: 152.000000
F:\golang>
```

In the above example, *"Liev"* is read as **string**, *18* is read as **int** and *152* is read as **float32**. This is how the assignment of input to variables happens:

fmt.Scanf("%s %d %f", &name, &age, &weight)

As mentioned earlier, the input is read according to the data type specified by verbs, no need arises to convert input from one form to another. Let us cross check this by writing a program to add two numbers. This time, we will insert \n between two verbs and hence, the user will have to hit enter after entering each number:

```
/*Scanf Add Two Numbers Demo*/
/*Package Declaration*/
package main
/*Import Statement - import fmt package*/
import ("fmt")
/*Mandatory main function*/
func main () {
```

```
/*Declare Variables*/
var num1, num2, sum int
/*Prompt the user to enter 2 numbers*/
fmt.Printf("\nEnter two numbers: ")
/*Read 2 numbers*/
fmt.Scanf("%d\n%d", &num1, &num2)
/*Calculate sum*/
sum = num1 + num2
/*Display everything*/
fmt.Printf("\nSum = %d\n", sum)
}
```

Output:

10.3 Reading Sentences

Both *Scanf* and *Scanln* function are not capable of reading sentences, i.e. strings containing words. There is a function called *ReadString* in the *bufio* package. Hence, *bufio* package needs to be included if you intend to use *ReadString* function. Alongside *bufio*, *os* should be imported as we need access to *os.Stdin* (standard input/output). Do not worry about the technicalities, this is an advanced topic. All you have to do is remember a few lines of code if you want to read a sentence. Here is the general syntax:

<Reader variable> := bufio.NewReader(os.Stdin)
<string variable>, _ := <Reader variable>.ReadString('\n')

Example:

r := bufio.NewReader(os.Stdin)

msg, _ := r.ReadString('\n')

Here is a program that prompts the user to enter something and reads a full sentence:

```
/*Read Sentence*/
/*Package Declaration*/
package main
/*Import Statement - import fmt, bufio, os package*/
import (
       "fmt"
       "bufio"
       "os"
       )
/*Mandatory main function*/
func main () {
/*Create an input reader variable of type NewReader
using stdin*/
    inputReader := bufio.NewReader(os.Stdin)
    /*Prompt the user to enter something*/
    fmt.Printf("\nEnter a sentence: ")
    /*Read using ReadString function*/
    text, _ := inputReader.ReadString('\n')
    /*Print whats been read*/
    fmt.Printf("\nYou have entered: \n%s", text)
    }
```

<u>Output:</u>

```
F:\golang>go build readsentence.go
F:\golang>readsentence.exe
Enter a sentence: Hello! This is a sentence.

You have entered:
Hello! This is a sentence.

F:\golang>_
```

11. Control Structures

Control structures are programming constructs used to give programmers better control over the flow of the program. When a program is compiled, an executable binary file is built. This file contains machine level instructions that are native to a particular platform. Every line of meaningful code results in one or more machine level instructions. For example, **var name string** will result in one type of a machine level instruction, **a = b + c** will result in another type of an instruction. This is done by the compiler and we do not have to worry about it. The point of bring this up in this chapter is to explain the flow of execution. So, back to the topic – each line of code refers to one or more executable instructions. Many lines of code will result in many machine level instructions. The executable binary once run will start executing from the first instruction till the last one. Conceptually, we can say that a program starts executing from the first line of code till the last one (although in reality the program file is not the one that executes, the executable binary does). The is a very linear flow of execution. We can alter this flow of execution using control structures. Go offers decision making constructs and loops as control structures.

11.1 Decision Making

Decision making constructs introduce conditionality to the execution of a program. For example, you can execute a block of code depending on whether a condition is met or not met. Go offers decision making constructs in the form of **if-else**, **switch** and some advanced constructs. We will take a look at *if-else* and *switch*.

11.1.1 If-Else construct

The *If-Else* construct is used to execute a block of code if a given condition is *true* and optionally execute a different block of code if the given condition is *false*. Let us begin with a simple if block. General syntax:

if (<condition>) {
/ *Statements to be executed if <condition> is true*/
}
Example:
if (num == 0) {
fmt.Println("num is 0")
}

An if statement should be given a condition to evaluate marked by *<condition>* in the above code snippet. This condition is usually a boolean expression which can evaluate to either *true* or *false*. If it evaluates to *true*, the statements inside the *if-block* (the block of code present within curly brackets after the *if statement*) will be executed. If it evaluates to *false*, the *if block* will be skipped and the program will resume execution from after the *if-block*.

Note: The condition can be a simple boolean expression such as *(a == 0)* or a combination of many boolean expressions using logical operators such as *(a != 0) && (b > 1)*.

Let us write a simple program which demonstrates the usage of an *if* statement:

```
/*If Demo*/
/*Package Declaration*/
package main
/*Import Statement - import fmt package*/
import ("fmt")
/*Mandatory main function*/
func main () {
    var a int = 20
    fmt.Printf("\nProgram    execution    begins.    This
statement is before the if block.\n")
    /*Check if a is greater than 10*/
    if (a > 10) {
        fmt.Printf("\nInside if block.\n%d is greater
than 10.\n", a)
    }
    fmt.Printf("\nOutside if block. Program coming to
an end.\n")
}
```

Output:

In this example, we had set a condition which evaluates to true and the *if-block* executes. Let us change the code, modify *if (a > 10)* to *if (a < 10)* and see what happens:

Output:

71

As seen, the statements inside the *if block* do not get executed when the given condition evaluates to *false*. It is possible to execute a different block of code when the given condition evaluates to false using an *else block*. The *else block* should immediately follow the *if block*. General syntax:

```
if (<condition>) {
/*Statements to be executed if <condition> is true*/
} else {
/*Statements to be executed if <condition> is false*/
}
Example:
if (num == 0) {
        fmt.Println("num is 0")
} else {
        fmt.Println("num is NOT 0")
}
```

The working of *if-else* construct is simple – if the condition evaluates to *true*, the *if block* will be executed and the *else block* will be skipped and if it evaluates to *false*, the *if block* will be skipped and the *else block* will be executed. Let us write a program using *if* and *else* blocks and see what happens when the given condition of the *if block* evaluates to *false*.

```
/*If Else Demo*/
/*Package Declaration*/
package main
/*Import Statement - import fmt package*/
import ("fmt")
/*Mandatory main function*/
func main () {
 var a int = 5
```

```
    fmt.Printf("\nProgram    execution    begins.    This
statement is before the if block.\n")
    /*Check if a is greater than 10*/
    if (a > 10) {
        fmt.Printf("\nInside  if  block.\n%d  is  greater
than 10.\n", a)
    } else {
        fmt.Printf("\nInside  else  block.\n%d  is  NOT
greater than 10.\n", a)
    }
    fmt.Printf("\nOutside    if/else    blocks.    Program
coming to an end.\n")
    }
```

Output:

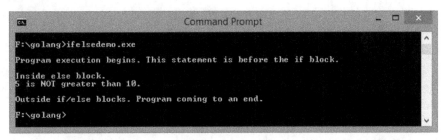

As seen, the condition *(a > 10)* evaluates to *false* as *a* is *5*. As a result, the *if block* gets skipped and the *else block* gets executed.

One *if-else block* combination will check for the validity of one condition. Depending on what the given condition evaluates to, either if or else block will get executed. If you want to check for more than one conditions, you can nest *if-else blocks* within *if-else blocks* like this:

if (<condition 1>) {

    */ *Statements to be executed if <condition 1> is true*/*

    if (<condition 2>) {

    */ *Statements to be executed if <condition 1> and <condition 2> are true*/*

```
        } else {
                /*Statements to be executed if <condition 1> is true and
<condition 2> is false*/
        }
    } else {
        /*Statements to be executed if <condition 1> is false*/
        if (<condition 3>) {
        /*Statements to be executed if <condition 1> is false and
<condition 3> is true*/
        } else {
                /*Statements to be executed if <condition 1> and
<condition 3> is false*/
        }
    }
```

Another way of checking for multiple conditions is by using **else-if blocks**. There will be a mandatory **if-block** and an optional **else-block**. Between these blocks, you can have as many **else-if** blocks as you want where each **else-if** statement will have its own condition. This way you can check for as many conditions as you want. Here is a general syntax:

```
if ( <condition 1>) {
        /* This block will be executed if <condition 1> is true. */
} else if ( <condition 2> ) {
/*This block will be executed if <condition 1> is false <condition 2>
is true */
} else if ( <condition 3> ) {
```

/*This block will be executed if <condition 1> and <condition 2> are false and <condition 3> is true.*/

```
} else {
```

/*This block will be executed if <condition 1>, <condition 2> and   *<condition 3> are false.*/*

```
}
```

When there is a combination of **if-else if-else** blocks, what happens is – the condition of the **if statement** will be checked. If that condition evaluates to **true**, the **if block** will be executed and that will be end of the story! <u>All the remaining blocks will be skipped</u>. However, if the condition evaluates to **false**, the execution control will jump to the **else if statement** that follows and its condition will be checked. If it evaluates to **true**, that particular **else if block** will be executed and rest of the blocks will be skipped. If its condition evaluates to **false**, the control will jump to the next **else-if block** (if present) and that block's condition will be checked. This process will continue until either a valid condition is found or there are no more **else-if blocks** left. If none of the conditions evaluate to **true**, the **else block** (if present) will be evaluated.

Let us write a Go program to check if a given number is positive, negative or zero:

```
/*Positive Negative Zero */
/*Package Declaration*/
package main
/*Import   Statement   -   import   fmt   and   strconv
package*/
import (
    "fmt"
    "strconv"
    )
/*Mandatory main function*/
```

```go
func main () {
    /*Declare variable to store input*/
    var num_str string
    fmt.Printf("\nEnter a number: ")
    /*Read user input using Scanln function*/
    fmt.Scanln(&num_str)
    /*Convert num_str to integer*/
    num, err := strconv.Atoi(num_str)
    /*Assign err to blank identifiers*/
    _ = err
    /*Check if num > 0*/
    if (num > 0) {
        fmt.Printf("\n%d is positive.\n", num)
    } else if (num < 0) {
        fmt.Printf("\n%d is negative.\n", num)
    } else {
        fmt.Printf("\n%d is zero.\n", num)
    }
}
```

Output:

```
C:\Windows\system32\cmd.exe

F:\golang>go build pnz.go
F:\golang>pnz.exe
Enter a number: 0
0 is zero.
F:\golang>pnz.exe
Enter a number: -685
-685 is negative.
F:\golang>pnz.exe
Enter a number: 175
175 is positive.
F:\golang>
```

11.1.2 Switch-Case construct

We have seen how to check for the validity of multiple conditions using multiple *else if* blocks. The *switch-case* construct provides even better better way of handling multiple conditions. There are multiple ways of writing a *switch-case* construct and we will take a look at a few important ones. Let us start with the basic format:

```
switch (<expression>) {
        case <constant expression 1>:
        /*Statements to be executed if <expression> matches <constant
expression 1>*/
        case <constant expression 2>:
        /*Statements to be executed if <expression> matches <constant
expression 2>*/
        case <constant expression 3>:
        /*Statements to be executed if <expression> matches <constant
expression 3>*/
        ...
        case <constant expression n>:
        /*Statements to be executed if <expression> matches <constant
expression n>*/
        default:
        /*Statements to be executed if <expression> finds no match*/
}
```

In this syntax of **switch-case** construct, the switch statement is given an expression to work with – marked by **<expression>** in the above code snippet. An expression can be something as simple as a variable. Inside the **switch** block, there are multiple **case** blocks where each **case statement** has a constant expression. When the **switch statement** is encountered, its expression is evaluated. The resulting value will be checked against the constant expressions of case blocks. If the resulting value matches one of the constant expressions, that particular ***case block*** is executed. This process is known as _testing for cases_. If the values does not match any of the constant expressions, the ***default*** case block (if present) is executed. Here is a simple ***switch-case*** demo:

```
/*Switch Demo 1*/
/*Package Declaration*/
package main
/*Import Statement - import fmt package*/
import ("fmt")
/*Mandatory main function*/
func main () {
 /*Create a variable for switch*/
 Option := 3
 /*Switch Option, where Option is int variable
assigned to 3*/
 switch (Option) {
     /*Various cases to match Option*/
     case 1:
         fmt.Printf("\nOption is 1.\n")
     case 2:
         fmt.Printf("\nOption is 2.\n")
     case 3:
         fmt.Printf("\nOption is 3.\n")
     /*Default case incase there is no match*/
     default:
         fmt.Printf("\nOption does not match any of
the cases.\n")
   }
  }
```

Output:

```
F:\golang>go build switchdemo1.go
F:\golang>switchdemo1.exe
Option is 3.
F:\golang>_
```

In the above program, there are 3 cases and the variable *Option* is used to switch. This variable has been assigned to 3, let us change *Option* to *1* and *9* and see what happens:

Output (Option = 1):

Output (Option = 9):

The variable used to switch can also be set in the **switch statement** itself as follows:

switch <optional statement, set variable>
(<variable/ expression>) {

  case <constant expression 1>:
  */ *Statements to be executed if <expression> matches <constant expression 1>*/*

  ...

  case <constant expression n>:
  */ *Statements to be executed if <expression> matches <constant expression n>*/*

  default:
  */ *Statements to be executed if <expression> finds no match*/*

}

Let us re-write the previous program and set *Option* to *2* in the switch statement itself:

```
/*Switch Demo 1*/
/*Package Declaration*/
package main
/*Import Statement - import fmt package*/
import ("fmt")
/*Mandatory main function*/
func main () {
/*Switch Option, where Option is int variable
short-declared and assigned to 2*/
    switch Option := 2
    (Option) {
        /*Various cases to match Option*/
        case 1:
            fmt.Printf("\nOption is 1.\n")
        case 2:
            fmt.Printf("\nOption is 2.\n")
        case 3:
            fmt.Printf("\nOption is 3.\n")
        /*Default case incase there is no match*/
        default:
            fmt.Printf("\nOption does not match any of
the cases.\n")
    }
}
```

Output:

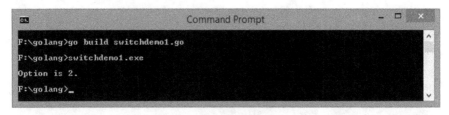

Another way of writing a *switch-case* construct is by using boolean expressions for each case statement as follows:

switch {

    case <boolean expression 1>:

/*Statements to be executed <boolean expression 1> evaluates to **true***/

case <boolean expression 2>:

/*Statements to be executed <boolean expression 2> evaluates to **true***/

case <boolean expression 3>:

/*Statements to be executed <boolean expression 3> evaluates to **true***/

...

case <boolean expression n>:

/*Statements to be executed <boolean expression n> evaluates to **true***/

default:

/*Statements to be executed if all boolean expressions are **false***/

}

Let us write a program to read a number from the user and check whether it is odd or even. We will use the *switch-case* syntax from the above code snippet:

```go
/*Switch Demo 2 -- Odd or Even*/
/*Package Declaration*/
package main
/*Import Statement - import fmt package*/
import ("fmt")
/*Mandatory main function*/
func main () {
 /*Declare a variable to store a number*/
 var num int
 /*Prompt the user to enter a number and read using
scanf*/
    fmt.Printf("\nEnter a number: ")
    fmt.Scanf("%d", &num)
    /*Switch num % 2*/
```

```
switch {
    /*Various cases for each outcome*/
    /*If the remainder is zero, the number is
even*/
    case (num % 2) == 0:
        fmt.Printf("\n%d is even.\n", num)
    /*If the remainder is one, the number is odd*/
    case (num % 2) == 1:
        fmt.Printf("\n%d is odd.\n", num)
}
}
```

Output:

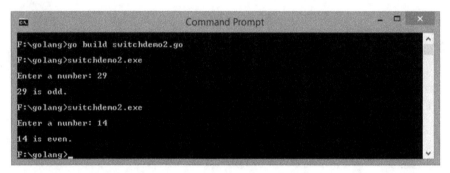

A *switch-case* construct can be used to switch using a variable of any basic data type, does not have to be a number. Let us write a program to ask the user to enter the name of a month and determine its serial number:

```
/*Switch Demo 3*/
/*Package Declaration*/
package main
/*Import Statement - import fmt package*/
import ("fmt")
/*Mandatory main function*/
func main () {
    /*Declare a variable to store the name of the
month*/
    var month string
    /*Prompt the user to enter the name of a month and
read using scanf*/
    fmt.Printf("\nEnter month: ")
    fmt.Scanf("%s", &month)
```

```go
    /*Switch month*/
    switch month {
        /*Various cases for each month*/
        case "January", "january":
            fmt.Printf("\nJanuary comes at No.1 in a
year.\n")
        case "February", "february":
            fmt.Printf("\nFebruary comes at No.2 in a
year.\n")
        case "March", "march":
            fmt.Printf("\nMarch comes at No.3 in a
year.\n")
        case "April", "april":
            fmt.Printf("\nApril comes at No.4 in a
year.\n")
        case "May", "may":
            fmt.Printf("\nMay comes at No.5 in a
year.\n")
        case "June", "june":
            fmt.Printf("\nJune comes at No.6 in a
year.\n")
        case "July", "july":
            fmt.Printf("\nJuly comes at No.7 in a
year.\n")
        case "August", "august":
            fmt.Printf("\nAugust comes at No.8 in a
year.\n")
        case "September", "september":
            fmt.Printf("\nSeptember comes at No.9 in a
year.\n")
        case "October", "october":
            fmt.Printf("\nOctober comes at No.10 in a
year.\n")
        case "November", "november":
            fmt.Printf("\nNovember comes at No.11 in a
year.\n")
        case "December", "december":
            fmt.Printf("\nDecember comes at No.12 in a
year.\n")
        /*Default case*/
        default:
            fmt.Printf("\n%s does not seem like the
name of a month!\n")
    }
    }
```

Output:

```
F:\golang>go build switchdemo3.go
F:\golang>switchdemo3.exe
Enter month: october
October comes at No.10 in a year.
F:\golang>switchdemo3.exe
Enter month: Sunday
Sunday does not seem like the name of a month!
F:\golang>switchdemo3.exe
Enter month: December
December comes at No.12 in a year.
F:\golang>switchdemo3.exe
Enter month: January
January comes at No.1 in a year.
F:\golang>
```

Refer to the program, notice how each case has two constant expressions. When you need to execute the same piece of code for more than one constant expressions, instead of writing a separate case with a different constant expression, you can write just one case statement with multiple constant expressions separated by comma.

11.2 Loops

A loop is a programming construct with which a piece of code can be run over and over again depending on whether or not a condition is met. Go offer only one loop called *for loop*.

11.2.1 for Loop

The basic syntax of for loop is as follows:

for <condition> {

*   /*Statements to be executed as long as <condition> is true*/*

}

Example:

num := 0

for num < 5 {

    fmt.Printf("num = %d", num)

    num = num + 1

}

When the execution control encounters a for loop, its condition is checked. If it evaluates to **true**, the statement inside the loop block are executed. This is one **loop iteration**. Once the end of the loop block is reached, the execution control will jump back to the **for statement** and check the condition again. If it evaluates to **true** again, the loop block will be executed once again. Such loop iterations will go on happening as long as the given condition evaluates to **true**. Once it evaluates to **false**, the execution control will come out of the loop. If the condition never becomes **false**, the loop will go on executing. Such a loop is known as an **infinite loop**.

Here is a program that prints 0 to 9 using a **for loop**:

```
/*For Demo 1*/
/*Package Declaration*/
package main
/*Import Statement - import fmt package*/
import ("fmt")
/*Mandatory main function*/
func main () {
 /*Initialize an integer variable to 0*/
 var count int = 0
 /*Run for loop from 0 to 9*/
 for (count < 10) {
    /*Print count*/
    fmt.Printf("count = %d\n", count)
    /*Increment count*/
    count++
 }
}
```

Output:

Another way of writing a for loop is by using a **_loop variable_**. Here is the general syntax:

for <loop variable initialization> ; <condition> ; <loop variable increment/decrement> {

/*Statements to be executed as long as <condition> is true*/

_}_

Using this syntax, you can initialize a loop variable in the **for statement** itself. It also gives you an option to increment/ decrement the loop variable. At the end of each iteration, the given condition will be checked. If it evaluates to **_true_**, the loop variable will be incremented/decremented and then loop block will be executed as the next iteration. The loop variable can also be short-declared in the **for statement** if it is not declared before. Using this syntax, let us write a program to print multiples of 5. The loop variable has been short-declared in the **for statement**.

```
/*For Demo 2*/
/*Package Declaration*/
package main
/*Import Statement - import fmt package*/
import ("fmt")
```

```
/*Mandatory main function*/
func main () {
 fmt.Printf("\nMultiples of 5\n\n")
 /*Run for loop from 1 to 10*/
 for count := 1 ; count <= 10 ; count++ {
    /*Print count * 5*/
    fmt.Printf("%d\n", count * 5)
 }
}
```

Output:

Here is an example where the loop variable has been previously declared:

```
/*For Demo 3*/
/*Package Declaration*/
package main
/*Import Statement - import fmt package*/
import ("fmt")
/*Mandatory main function*/
func main () {
 /*Declare an int variable*/
 var count int
 fmt.Printf("\nMultiples of 3\n\n")
 /*Run for loop from 1 to 20*/
 for count = 1 ; count <= 20 ; count++ {
    /*Print count * 3*/
    fmt.Printf("%d\n", count * 3)
 }
}
```

Output:

```
F:\golang>go build fordemo3.go
F:\golang>fordemo3.exe
Multiples of 3

3
6
9
12
15
18
21
24
27
30
33
36
39
42
45
48
51
54
57
60
F:\golang>
```

11.2.2 Control Statements

As long as the given condition is *true*, a loop will go on executing. This is the normal execution process of a loop. It is possible to alter this flow of execution of a loop using control statements such as *continue* and *break*.

11.2.2.1 continue statement

When a *continue* statement is encountered, the execution control jumps to the beginning of the loop thereby skipping all the statements after the *continue* statement. In other words, the loop moves to the next iteration. Let us write a program to print only odd numbers between 1 and 30:

```
/*For Demo -- continue */
/*Package Declaration*/
package main
/*Import Statement - import fmt package*/
import ("fmt")
```

```
/*Mandatory main function*/
func main () {
 fmt.Printf("\nOdd numbers between 1 and 30\n\n")
 /*Run for loop from 1 to 30*/
 for count := 1 ; count <= 30 ; count++ {
     if (count % 2 == 0) {
         continue
     }
     fmt.Printf("%d\n", count)
 }
}
```

Output:

```
F:\golang>go build continuedemo.go
F:\golang>continuedemo.exe
Odd numbers between 1 and 30
1
3
5
7
9
11
13
15
17
19
21
23
25
27
29
F:\golang>
```

11.2.2.2 break statement

When a *break* statement is encountered, the execution of the loop halts and the control comes out of the loop. Let us understand this concept with a programming example. We shall run a loop from 1 to 10 and break out of the loop when count becomes 7:

```
/*For Demo -- break */
/*Package Declaration*/
package main
/*Import Statement - import fmt package*/
import ("fmt")
/*Mandatory main function*/
func main () {
```

```
/*Run for loop from 1 to 10*/
for count := 1 ; count <= 10 ; count++ {
    if (count == 7) {
        break
    }
    fmt.Printf("count = %d\n", count)
}
}
```

Output:

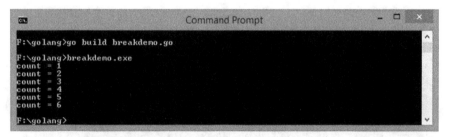

A more practical use of the **break** statement can be understood with the help of the following program where we ask the user to enter a number and determine whether it is prime or composite:

```
/*Prime or composite - using break*/
/*Package Declaration*/
package main
/*Import Statement - import fmt package*/
import ("fmt")
/*Mandatory main function*/
func main () {
/*Declare variable to store user input and to serve
as loop counter*/
    var i, num int
/*Prompt the user to enter a number and read using
Scanf*/
    fmt.Printf("\nEnter a number: ")
    fmt.Scanf("%d", &num)
/*Run loop from 2 to num as every number is
divisible by 1*/
    for i = 2 ; i <= num ; i ++ {
        if (num % i == 0) {
            break
        }
    }
```

```
    if (num != i) {
        fmt.Printf("\n%d   is   a   composite   number.\n",
num)
    } else {
        fmt.Printf("\n%d is a prime number.\n", num)
    }
}
```

Output:

Let us write a few more programs to gain better understanding of loops. Following is a program that calculates factorial of a given number. Factorial of a number *n* is represented as $n! = n \times (n-1) \times (n-2) \times \ldots \times 1$. Factorial of a negative number cannot be calculated and the factorial of zero is 1.

```
/*Factorial*/
/*Package Declaration*/
package main
/*Import Statement - import fmt package*/
import ("fmt")
/*Mandatory main function*/
func main () {
    /*Declare   variable   to   store   user   input,   loop
counter and factorial*/
    var i, num int
    var f int = 1
    /*Prompt the user to enter a number and read using
Scanf*/
    fmt.Printf("\nEnter a number: ")
```

91

```
    fmt.Scanf("%d", &num)
    /*Run loop from num to 1*/
    for i = num ; i > 0 ; i -- {
        f = f * i
    }
    if (num >= 0) {
        fmt.Printf("\nFactorial of %d is %d\n", num, f)
    } else {
        fmt.Printf("\nFactorial of a negative number
cannot be calculated\n")
    }
}
```

<u>Output:</u>

Let us write another program using loops where we will calculate the sum of first *n* even numbers.

```
/*Sum of n even numbers*/
/*Package Declaration*/
package main
/*Import Statement - import fmt package*/
import ("fmt")
/*Mandatory main function*/
func main () {
    /*Declare variable to store n, loop counter and
sum*/
    var i, n int
```

```
    var even_num, sum int = 1, 0
    /*Prompt the user to enter a number and read using
Scanf*/
    fmt.Printf("\nEnter n: ")
    fmt.Scanf("%d", &n)
    fmt.Printf("\nFirst %d even numbers: \n\n", n)
    for i = 1 ; even_num <= n ; i ++ {
        if (i % 2 == 0) {
            fmt.Printf("%d ", i)
            sum += i
            even_num++
        }
    }
    fmt.Printf("\n\nSum of above even numbers: %d\n",
sum)
    }
```

Output:

12. Arrays

An array is a collection of similar items. In programmatic terms, an array in Go language is a data structure which contains items of the *same data type*. Each item inside an array is known as an *array element* (or just an *element*). An element can be referred to using its position in the array which is known as an *index*. An array index begins at *0* and ends at *one less than the size of the array (size – 1)*. For example, if we had an array of 10 elements, the first element of that array would be present at 0, the second one at index 1, the third one at index 2, ..., and the last element would be present at index 9.

In Go programming language, an array can be declared using the following syntax:

var <array variable> [<size of the array>] <data type>
Example:
var array1 [5] int
var msg [3] string
var x [10] float64

Once an array is declared, its elements will get *zero-values* (numeric arrays will hold 0 and string arrays will hold empty strings). Individual elements can be accessed using their indexes enclosed with the *access operator ([ ])*. This way, you can set (and also retrieve/print) individual elements of an array. Here is an example:

/ *Declaring an int array of size 5. First index is 0, last index is 4*/
var num_array [5] int

/*Setting element at index 0 to 15*/

num_array[0] = 15

/*Setting element at index 1 to -35*/

num_array[1] = -35

/*Setting element at index 2 to 0*/

num_array[2] = 0

/*Setting element at index 3 to 68*/

num_array[3] = 68

/*Setting element at index 4 to 18*/

num_array[4] = 18

This is how **num_array** will look inside memory:

		num_array			
Elements =>	15	-35	0	68	18
Index =>	0	1	2	3	4

We will now write a program where in we will create an integer array, set element values and print them back. The whole array can be printed using the verbs **%v** or **%d**. Printing individual elements would be the same as printing any other integer variable:

```
/*Array Demo 1*/
/*Package Declaration*/
package main
/*Import Statement - import fmt package*/
import ("fmt")
/*Mandatory main function*/
func main () {
 /*Declare an array of 7 integers*/
 var arr [7] int
 /*Set values of all elements*/
 arr[0] = 83
 arr[1] = -34
 arr[2] = 55
```

```
arr[3] = 97
arr[4] = -24
arr[5] = -11
arr[6] = 46
/*Print the whole array*/
fmt.Printf("\nArray arr:\n\n%v\n", arr)
/*Print index and corresspoiding values*/
fmt.Printf("\nValue at index: 0 ==> %d", arr[0])
fmt.Printf("\nValue at index: 1 ==> %d", arr[1])
fmt.Printf("\nValue at index: 2 ==> %d", arr[2])
fmt.Printf("\nValue at index: 3 ==> %d", arr[3])
fmt.Printf("\nValue at index: 4 ==> %d", arr[4])
fmt.Printf("\nValue at index: 5 ==> %d", arr[5])
fmt.Printf("\nValue at index: 6 ==> %d\n", arr[6])
}
```

Output:

It is also possible to initialize an array at the time of declaration using the following syntax:

var <array variable> = [<optional size>] <data type> {<elements separated by comma>}

Example:

var arr1 = [] int {-3, 0, 3}

var arr2 = [6] float32 {0.36, -0.25, 0.01, -0.67, 0.88, 0.73}

Here is a program that demonstrates array initialization:

```go
/*Array Demo 2*/
/*Package Declaration*/
package main
/*Import Statement - import fmt package*/
import ("fmt")
/*Mandatory main function*/
func main () {
 /*Declare an array of 5 floats and initialize*/
 var arr = [5] float32 {4.6, -65.21, 0.64, -12.76,
25.75}
 /*Print the whole array*/
 fmt.Printf("\nArray arr:\n\n%v\n", arr)
 /*Print index and corresspoiding values*/
 fmt.Printf("\nValue at index: 0 ==> %f", arr[0])
 fmt.Printf("\nValue at index: 1 ==> %f", arr[1])
 fmt.Printf("\nValue at index: 2 ==> %f", arr[2])
 fmt.Printf("\nValue at index: 3 ==> %f", arr[3])
 fmt.Printf("\nValue at index: 4 ==> %f\n", arr[4])
 }
```

Output:

```
F:\golang>go build arraydemo2.go

F:\golang>arraydemo2.exe

Array arr:

[4.6 -65.21 0.64 -12.76 25.75]

Value at index: 0 ==> 4.600000
Value at index: 1 ==> -65.209999
Value at index: 2 ==> 0.640000
Value at index: 3 ==> -12.760000
Value at index: 4 ==> 25.750000

F:\golang>
```

An array can be of any data type. When initializing an array, the size may or may not be specified. It will be taken automatically depending on the number of elements you set at the time of initialization. At any point in the program, you can use the function *len(<array variable)* to determine the size of an array. Also, accessing elements every time manually may not be the best way – loops do a great job working with arrays. Here is an example that demonstrates these concepts:

```
/*Array Demo 3*/
/*Package Declaration*/
package main
/*Import Statement - import fmt package*/
import ("fmt")
/*Mandatory main function*/
func main () {
 /*Declare an array of 10 strings and initialize*/
 var country = [] string {"USA", "UK", "India",
"Brazil", "South Africa", "Argentina", "New Zealand",
"Russia", "Morocco", "Latvia"}
 /*Print the whole array*/
 fmt.Printf("\nArray country:\n\n%v\n", country)
 /*Print index and corresponding values using for
loop*/
 /*Use len function to retrieve the size of the
array*/
 size := len(country)
 for i := 0 ; i < size ; i ++ {
     fmt.Printf("\nValue at index: %d ==> %s", i,
country[i])
 }
 fmt.Printf("\n")
 }
```

Output:

Let us take a few more programming examples to better understand arrays. Here is an example that takes 5 integers as input from the user and saves it in an array, calculates the sum and average of those integers:

```
/*Array Input*/

/*Package Declaration*/
package main
/*Import Statement - import fmt package*/
import (
        "fmt"
        "strconv"
        )
/*Mandatory main function*/
func main () {
 /*Declare variables*/
 var arr [5] int
 var sum int = 0
 var num_str string
 /*Declare a variable to store average*/
 var avg float32
 /*Prompt the user to enter 5 elements, use for
loop*/
    for i := 0 ; i < 5 ; i++ {
        fmt.Printf("\nEnter element at index %d: ", i)
        fmt.Scanln(&num_str)
        /*Convert num_str to integer*/
        num, err := strconv.Atoi(num_str)
        /*Assign num to arr[i]*/
        arr[i] = num
        /*Assign err to blank identifier*/
        _ = err
        /*Keep calculating sum*/
        sum += arr[i]
    }
    /*Calculate average*/
    avg = float32 (sum) / 5.0
    fmt.Printf("\nArray   arr:\n%v\nSum:   %d\nAverage:
%f\n", arr, sum, avg)
    }
```

Let us write a program to take 5 integers as input from the user, save them in an array and reverse the array:

```
/*Reverse an array*/
/*Package Declaration*/
package main

/*Import Statement - import fmt, strconv package*/
import (
    "fmt"
    "strconv"
    )
/*Mandatory main function*/
func main () {
 /*Declare variables*/
 var arr [5] int
 var num_str string
 /*Prompt the user to enter 5 elements, use for
loop*/
 for i := 0 ; i < 5 ; i++ {
     fmt.Printf("\nEnter element at index %d: ", i)
     fmt.Scanln(&num_str)
     /*Convert num_str to integer*/
     num, err := strconv.Atoi(num_str)
     /*Assign num to arr[i]*/
     arr[i] = num
     /*Assign err to blank identifier*/
     _ = err
 }
 fmt.Printf("\nOriginal array:\n%v\n", arr)
```

```
/*Reverse Array*/
for i := 0 ; i < 5/2 ; i++ {
    temp := arr[i]
    arr[i] = arr[4-i]
    arr[4-i] = temp
}
fmt.Printf("\nReversed array:\n%v\n", arr)
}
```

Output:

```
                              Command Prompt                    - □  x

F:\golang>go build arrayrev.go

F:\golang>arrayrev.exe

Enter element at index 0: 8

Enter element at index 1: 2

Enter element at index 2: 0

Enter element at index 3: 3

Enter element at index 4: 9

Original array:
[8 2 0 3 9]

Reversed array:
[9 3 0 2 8]

F:\golang>
```

13. Functions

A function is a piece of reusable code that can be *"called"* to perform certain tasks. We have already used a few functions such as *Printf, Scalnln, Atoi, etc.* These functions are written by someone else and we are using them to make our programming life easier. *Scanln* and *Println* are I/O functions which implicitly work with the devices (either directly or indirectly) to do the required job. Imagine how inconvenient programming would be if we had to write a big piece of code every time we wanted to print something on the console. Because *Println* and *Scanln* functions are already defined somewhere by someone, programmers like us can simply call them to get our job done. In this chapter, we will learn to write our own functions.

The topic of functions can be broadly classified into two categories – *function definition* and *function call.*

13.1 Function Definition

Function definition is a piece of code that defines what a function does. For example, a function to add two number will have the logic to add to numbers in its function definition. A program can have zero or more user defined functions. *All functions should be defined outside the main function.* The best place to define functions is between the package declaration statement and main function. Here is a general syntax of function definition:

func <function name> (<arguments>) <return type> {

```
    /*Function Body*/
    //Statements
}
Example:
func helloFunction () {
        fmt.Printf("\nHello! We are inside helloFunction!\n")
}
```

Here are the parts of a basic function definition:

- **Function Name**

  - A function name is the name given to a function marked by *<function name>* in the above code snippet. This name is used to identify and call the function. Function naming rules are the same as identifier/variable naming rules.

- **Arguments**

  - Arguments (marked by *<arguments>* in the above code snippet) are the values that a function *"accepts"* into local variables. These values are passed to a function at the time of function call. A function may accept zero or more arguments. When there are more than one arguments, they should be separated using comma. Arguments are also called *Parameters*.

- **Return Type**

  - A function can optionally return a value back to the calling function. The data type of the value that a particular function is returning should be specified in the return type field marked by **<return type>** in the above code snippet.

- **Function Body**

  - Function body is the core part of a function where the actual work gets done. If you have a function to calculate the factorial of a given number, the code that is responsible for calculating factorial of a number goes in this part of the definition.

Here are a few code snippets that show different types of functions:

```
/*Function that accepts no arguments and returns no value*/
func sayHello () {
  fmt.Printf("\nJust a function that prints Hello on the console.")
}
/*Function that accepts one augment and returns no value*/
func showValue (name string) {
  fmt.Printf("\nReceived name = %s", name)
}
/*Function that accepts one argument and returns one value*/
func doubleIt(x int) int {
  return (x * 2)
}
/*Function that accepts three arguments and returns two values*/
func doMath (a int, b int, c int) (int, float32) {
  sum := a + b + c
  avg = float32 (sum) / 3.0
  return sum, avg
}
```

13.2 Function Call

A defined function will not execute on its own. It needs to be called (from another function, perhaps from the main function). A function is called with the help of its name while passing the exact number of arguments (in correct order) as defined in the function definition. Here is the general syntax:

<function name>(<arguments>)
Example:
myFunction( )

Let us make calls to each of the functions defined in the previous section:

sayHello()
showValue("Sarah")
x = doubleIt(100)
sum, avg = doMath (1, 2, 3)

Here is a simple function that accepts no arguments and returns no value:

```
/*Function Demo 1*/
/*Package Declaration*/
package main
/*Import Statement - import fmt package*/
import ("fmt")
/*User defined function*/
/*This function accepts no arguments and returns no
value*/
func myFunction () {
  fmt.Printf("\n[Inside myFunction] - Hello! from
myFunction\n")
  }
/*Mandatory main function*/
func main () {
```

```
    fmt.Printf("\n[Inside    main]    -    now    calling
myFunction\n")
    /*Call myFunction*/
    myFunction()
    fmt.Printf("\n[Inside main] - reaching the end of
main function/program\n")
    }
```

Output:

```
C:\Windows\system32\cmd.exe
F:\golang>go build functions1.go
F:\golang>functions1.exe
[Inside main] - now calling myFunction
[Inside myFunction] - Hello! from myFunction
[Inside main] - reaching the end of main function/program
F:\golang>
```

13.3 Passing Arguments to Functions

Arguments can be passed to a function at the time of function call by enclosing them within brackets. Multiple arguments can be passed by separating them using commas. Arguments can only be passed to those functions which accept arguments. One important thing to note here is that the number and the order of arguments passed during a function call should be the same as defined in the function definition. Here is a Go program that demonstrates the working of a function that accepts two integers and calculates their sum:

```
/*Function Demo 2*/
/*Package Declaration*/
package main
/*Import Statement - import fmt package*/
import ("fmt")
/*User defined function*/
/*This function accepts 2 arguments and returns no
value*/
```

```
func addTwoNumbers (a int, b int) {
  sum := a + b
  fmt.Printf("\n[Inside addTwoNumbers] - Received two
arguments: \n\na = %d, b = %d\n\n", a, b)
  fmt.Printf("\n[Inside addTwoNumbers] - Sum = %d\n",
sum)
  }
  /*Mandatory main function*/
  func main () {
    fmt.Printf("\n[Inside    main]    -    now    calling
addTwoNumbers, passing 5 and 9 as arguments\n")
    /*Call addTwoNumbers*/
    addTwoNumbers(5, 9)
    fmt.Printf("\n[Inside main] - reaching the end of
main function/program\n")
  }
```

Output:

13.4 Returning Values

A function can return values back to the calling function with the help of a return statement. Here is the general syntax:

return <values>

Example:

*/*Single value*/*

return name

*/*Multiple values*/*

return x, y, z

When calling a function that returns a value, a variable must be specified to receive the returned value otherwise it will be lost. When receiving multiple values, multiple variables should be specified – multiple assignment will be performed when multiple values are returned. Here are a few examples:

*/ *Receive single value*/*
name = getName()
*/ *Receive multiple values*/*
a, b, c = getValues()

Let us write a function to accept three integers, calculate their average and return it:

```
/*Function Demo 3*/

/*Package Declaration*/
package main
/*Import Statement - import fmt package*/
import ("fmt")
/*User defined function*/
/*This function accepts 3 arguments and returns one
value*/
func findAverage (a int, b int, c int) float32 {
    fmt.Printf("\n[Inside findAverage] - Received three
arguments: \n\na = %d, b = %d, c = %d\n\n", a, b, c)
    /*Calculate sum*/
    sum := a + b + c
    /*Calculate average, use type casting to convert
from int to float*/
    avg := (float32 (sum) / 3.0)
    fmt.Printf("\n[Inside findAverage] - Returning avg
back to main\n")
    return avg
}
/*Mandatory main function*/
func main () {
```

```
    fmt.Printf("\n[Inside     main]     -    now    calling
findAverage, passing 2, 8 and -3 as arguments\n")
    /*Call  findAverage,  receive  returned  value  in
average variable (short declared)*/
    average := findAverage(2, 8, -3)
    fmt.Printf("\n[Inside   main]   -   average   =   %f\n",
average)
    fmt.Printf("\n[Inside   main]  -  reaching  the  end  of
main function/program\n")
    }
```

Output:

Let us write another program to demonstrate the working of a function which returns multiple values. We will define a function to accept two integers and return four values – sum, difference, product and quotient:

```
/*Function Demo 4*/
/*Package Declaration*/
package main
/*Import Statement - import fmt package*/
import ("fmt")
/*User defined function*/
/*This function accepts 2 arguments and returns 4
values*/
func performArithmetics (a int, b int) (int, int,
int, float32) {
    fmt.Printf("\n[Inside     performArithmetics]     -
Received 2 arguments: \n\na = %d, b = %d\n\n", a, b)
    /*Calculate sum, diff, prod, quo*/
    sum := a + b
```

```
diff := a - b
prod := a * b
quo := float32 (a) / float32 (b)
fmt.Printf("\n[Inside        performArithmetics]     -
Returning sum, diff, prod, quo back to main\n")
return sum, diff, prod, quo
}
/*Mandatory main function*/
func main () {
/*Declare variables to store return values*/
var sum, diff, prod int
var quo float32
fmt.Printf("\n[Inside   main]    -    now    calling
performArithmetics, passing 15 and 6 as arguments\n")
/*Call performArithmetics, receive returned values
in sum, diff, prod, quo*/
sum, diff, prod, quo = performArithmetics(15, 6)
fmt.Printf("\n[Inside main] - sum = %d, diff = %d,
prod = %d, quo = %f\n", sum, diff, prod, quo)
fmt.Printf("\n[Inside main] - reaching the end of
main function/program\n")
}
```

Output:

```
C:\Windows\system32\cmd.exe

F:\golang>go build functions4.go
F:\golang>functions4.exe
[Inside main] - now calling performArithmetics, passing 15 and 6 as arguments
[Inside performArithmetics] - Received 2 arguments:
a = 15, b = 6

[Inside performArithmetics] - Returning sum, diff, prod, quo back to main
[Inside main] - sum = 21, diff = 9, prod = 90, quo = 2.500000
[Inside main] - reaching the end of main function/program
F:\golang>_
```

13.5 Passing Arrays as Arguments

The procedure of passing arrays to functions as arguments is the same as passing any other argument. Here is a general syntax:

func <function name> (<array variable>[ ] <data type>) <return type> {

    /*Statements*/

}

/*OR*/

func <function name> (<array variable>[<size>] <data type>) <return type> {

    /*Statements*/

}

Example:

    func demoFunction (names [ ] string) {

        /*Statements*/

    }

    /*OR*/

    func demoFunction (names [10] string) {

        /*Statements*/

    }

Note: It is always advisable to mention the size of the array although, the program will work fine without it in most cases.

Let a write a Go program to accept an integer array and return the sum of all elements and their average:

```
/*Function Demo 5*/
/*Package Declaration*/
package main
/*Import Statement - import fmt package*/
import ("fmt")
/*User defined function*/
/*This function accepts an array as an argument and
returns 2 values*/
func getSumAvg (arr[10] int) ( int, float32) {
```

```go
    fmt.Printf("\n[Inside getSumAvg]  -  Received 1
argument: \n\narr[10] = %v\n\n", arr)
    /*Calculate sum, avg*/
    sum := 0
    for i := 0 ; i < 10 ; i++ {
        /*Keep calculating sum*/
        sum += arr[i]
    }
    /*Calculate average*/
    avg := float32 (sum) / 10.0
    fmt.Printf("\n[Inside getSumAvg] - Returning sum,
avg back to main\n")
    return sum, avg
    }


    /*Mandatory main function*/
    func main () {
    /*Declare an integer array of 10 elements*/
    var arr = [10] int {9, -5, 6, 12, -3, 4, -1, -1,
25, 10}
    /*Declare variables to store sum and average*/
    var sum int
    var avg float32
    fmt.Printf("\n[Inside  main]  -  now  calling
getSumAvg, passing arr = %v as an argument\n", arr)
    /*Call getSumAvg, receive returned values in sum,
avg*/
    sum, avg = getSumAvg(arr)
    fmt.Printf("\n[Inside main] - sum = %d, avg =
%f\n", sum, avg)
    fmt.Printf("\n[Inside main] - reaching the end of
main function/program\n")
    }
```

Output:

113

14. Strings

A string is a sequence of characters. A constant string can be formed by enclosing a sequence of characters inside double quotes. Just like an array, individual characters can be accessed with the help of the *access operator ([ ])* by specifying their indexes. Index of a string begins at *0* and ends at *one less than the size of the string*. The length of a string can be determined using the *len(<string>)* function. Using the access operator, the individual characters can only be read but not set. Here is a simple Go program the demonstrates these string basics:

```
/*String Demo 1*/
/*Package Declaration*/
package main
/*Import Statement - import fmt package*/
import ("fmt")
/*Mandatory main function*/
func main () {
 /*Declare and initialize a string*/
 var name string = "Monica"
 /*Fetch length of the string*/
 length := len(name)
 /*Display the string and its length*/
 fmt.Printf("\nname  =  %s,  length  =  %d\n",  name,
length)
 /*Use for loop to print individual characters of
the string*/
 for i:= 0 ; i < length ; i++ {
     fmt.Printf("\nCharacter at index %d ==> %c\n",
i, name[i])
 }
}
```

Output:

```
F:\golang>go build stringdemo1.go
F:\golang>stringdemo1.exe
name = Monica, length = 6
Character at index 0 ==> M
Character at index 1 ==> o
Character at index 2 ==> n
Character at index 3 ==> i
Character at index 4 ==> c
Character at index 5 ==> a
F:\golang>
```

Individual characters of a string can be fetched into a character array using the *rune* functions as follows:

<character array var> = []rune(<String>)

Example:

c_arr = []rune(str)

An array of characters can be converted to a string using the *string* function as follows:

<string> = string (<character array variable>)

str = string (char_array)

Here is a program that demonstrates the working of this function:

```go
/*Rune demo*/
/*Package Declaration*/
package main
/*Import Statement - import fmt package*/
import ("fmt")
/*Mandatory main function*/
func main () {
 str := "Excelsior"
 str_length := len(str)
 /*Use rune to fetchs characters in an array*/
 str_char := []rune(str)
```

```
    fmt.Printf("\nstr:    %s,   length:    %d",    str,
str_length)
    fmt.Printf("\n\nCharacter array: %c\n", str_char)
    fmt.Printf("\nstr_char  character  array  elements:
\n")
    for i:= 0 ; i < str_length ; i++ {
        fmt.Printf("\nCharacter  at  index  %d  ==>  %c\n",
i, str_char[i])
    }
}
```

Output:

There is a package called **strings** which has many built-in functions that help in string manipulations. Let us take a look at a few important ones:

14.1 Concatenating strings

Two or more strings can be concatenated using the **strings.Join** function. In order to do so, the strings to be concatenated should be placed inside a string array. Here is the general syntax:

strings.Join(<string array>, <separator>)

Example:

big_string := *strings.Join(arr, " ")*

There is an even simpler way of concatenating two or more strings – using the **+ operator**. General syntax:

<concatenated string variable> = <string 1> + <string 2> + ... <string n>

Example:

big_str := "hello" + " " + "world!"

Let us write a program that demonstrates both these concatenation methods:

```
/*String Demo 2 - Concatenation*/
/*Package Declaration*/
package main
/*Import Statement - import fmt, strings packages*/
import (
    "fmt"
    "strings"
    )
/*Mandatory main function*/
func main () {
  /*Declare and initialize a string array*/
  var words = [] string {"This", "is", "an", "array",
"of", "7", "strings"}
  /*Display the string array*/
  fmt.Printf("\nwords array: %s\n", words)
  /*Concatenate using strings.Join*/
  words_str := strings.Join (words, " ")
  fmt.Printf("\nConcatenated      string      (using
strings.Join): %s\n", words_str)
  /*Short declare some strings*/
  str1 := "Go"
  str2 := "Programming"
  str3 := "Language"
  /*Concatenate str1, str2 and str3*/
  str4 := str1 + " " + str2 + " " + str3
```

```
    fmt.Printf("\nstr1   =   %s\nstr2   =   %s\nstr3   =
%s\n\nConcatenated string (using + operator)\n\nstr4 =
%s\n", str1, str2, str3, str4)

    }
```

Output:

14.2 Compare strings

The ***Compare*** function from the ***strings*** package is used to compare two strings. Syntax:

strings.Compare(<string1>, <string2>)

Example:

result := (string1, string2)

This function returns *0* is both strings are the same, returns *-1* if ***string1*** is lexicographically less than ***string2*** and returns *1* if ***string1*** is lexicographically greater than ***string2***. Let us write a program to read two strings from the user and compare them:

```
/*Compare two strings*/
/*Package Declaration*/
package main
/*Import Statement - import fmt, bufio, os, strings
package*/
    import (
```

```
        "fmt"
        "bufio"
        "os"
        "strings"
        )
    /*Mandatory main function*/
    func main () {
    /*Create an input reader variable of type NewReader
using stdin*/
    inputReader := bufio.NewReader(os.Stdin)
    /*Prompt the user to enter something*/
    fmt.Printf("\nEnter a string: ")
    /*Read string using ReadString function*/
    str1, _ := inputReader.ReadString('\n')
    fmt.Printf("\nEnter another string: ")
    /*Read string using ReadString function*/
    str2, _ := inputReader.ReadString('\n')
    /*Compare str1 and str2 using strings.Compare*/
    result := strings.Compare(str1, str2)
    if (result == 0) {
        fmt.Printf("\nBoth strings are the same.\n")
    } else if (result > 0) {
        fmt.Printf("\nFirst string is lexicographically
greater than the second string.\n")
    } else {
        fmt.Printf("\nSecond                string          is
lexicographically greater than the first string.\n")
    }
    }
```

Output:

120

14.3 Search for a string inside another string

The **Contains** function from the strings package is used to check if a string is present in another string. This function returns boolean **true** if the string is present and returns **false** if absent. Syntax:

strings.Compare(<main string>, <string to be searched>)

Example:

result := ("Hello World", "World")

Further, you can use **IndexOf** function from the **strings** package to determine the first occurrence of the given string in the main string. This function function return **-1** if the string is not present in the main string. Here is a program that reads two strings from the user and searches for the second string in the main string:

```go
/*Search for a string within another string*/
/*Package Declaration*/
package main
/*Import Statement - import fmt, bufio, os, strings
package*/
import (
        "fmt"
        "bufio"
        "os"
        "strings"
        )
/*Mandatory main function*/
func main () {
    /*Create an input reader variable of type NewReader
using stdin*/
    inputReader := bufio.NewReader(os.Stdin)
    /*Prompt the user to enter something*/
    fmt.Printf("\nEnter the main string: ")
    /*Read string using ReadString function*/
    main_str, _ := inputReader.ReadString('\n')
    fmt.Printf("\nEnter the string to be searched
inside the main string: ")
```

```
    /*Read string using ReadString function*/
    str, _ := inputReader.ReadString('\n')
    /*Use trim function to remove all \n and \r
characters*/
    str = strings.Trim(str, "\n\r")
    result := strings.Contains(main_str, str)
    if (result == true) {
        fmt.Printf("\nThe given string is present in
the main string.")
        /*Find the first occurrence*/
        first := strings.Index(main_str, str)
        /*Print first index*/
        fmt.Printf("\n\nFirst Occurrence: %d\n", first)

    } else {
        fmt.Printf("\nThe given string is not present
in the main string.\n")
    }
}
```

Output:

14.4 Trimming a string

There may arise a need to remove unwanted character from a string. You can use the *Trim* function from the strings package as follows:

<trimmed_string> = *strings.Trim(<string>, <character set to be trimmed>)*

When reading strings from the user, there is a high chance that *\n* or *\r* or both get appended to the string. You can use the **Trim** function to remove these characters:

new_str = strings.Trim(str, "\n\r")

In fact, let us see what happens when we read a string from the user – we will convert the string to character array to take a look at each character:

```
/*Pre-trim demo*/
/*Package Declaration*/
package main
/*Import Statement - import fmt, bufio, os, strings
package*/
    import (
        "fmt"
        "bufio"
        "os"
        )
/*Mandatory main function*/
func main () {
    /*Create an input reader variable of type NewReader
using stdin*/
    inputReader := bufio.NewReader(os.Stdin)
    /*Prompt the user to enter something*/
    fmt.Printf("\nEnter a string: ")
    /*Read string using ReadString function*/
    str, _ := inputReader.ReadString('\n')
    str_length := len(str)
    fmt.Printf("\nLength: %d", str_length)
    /*Use rune to fetchs characters in an array*/
    str_char := []rune(str)
    fmt.Printf("\n\nCharacter   array:   \n   %c   \n",
str_char)
    for i:= 0 ; i < str_length ; i++ {
        fmt.Printf("\nCharacter at  index %d ==> %c\n",
i, str_char[i])
    }
}
```

Output:

```
F:\golang>go build pretrin.go
F:\golang>pretrin.exe
Enter a string: Linux
Length: 7
Character array:
 [L i n u x
]
Character at index 0 ==> L
Character at index 1 ==> i
Character at index 2 ==> n
Character at index 3 ==> u
Character at index 4 ==> x
Character at index 5 ==>
Character at index 6 ==>

F:\golang>
```

We entered the word Linux, which clearly has 5 characters. But the length is reflected as 7. Also, while printing characters, we see two empty characters at location 5 and 7. Let us do a bit of investigation and see what is going on. We will modify the following statement:

```
fmt.Printf("\nCharacter at index %d ==> %c\n", i, str_char[i])
```

To:

```
fmt.Printf("\nCharacter at index %d ==> %X\n", i, str_char[i])
```

The new statement will print the HEX code of the characters. Here is the new output:

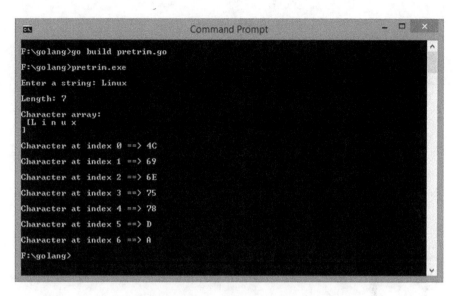

Character at *index 5* is *D* which is *0x0D* and at *index 6* is *A* which is *0x0A*. If you cross check these *HEX* values in an *ASCII* table, you will realize that these characters are \r and \n respectively. Let us use the *Trim* function and see what happens. Here is the new program:

```
/*Trim demo*/
/*Package Declaration*/
package main
/*Import Statement - import fmt, bufio, os, strings
package*/
import (
        "fmt"
        "bufio"
        "os"
        "strings"
        )
/*Mandatory main function*/
func main () {
  /*Create an input reader variable of type NewReader
using stdin*/
    inputReader := bufio.NewReader(os.Stdin)
    /*Prompt the user to enter something*/
    fmt.Printf("\nEnter a string: ")
    /*Read string using ReadString function*/
```

```
str, _ := inputReader.ReadString('\n')
/*Trim to remove unwanted characters*/
str = strings.Trim(str, "\n\r")
str_length := len(str)
fmt.Printf("\nLength: %d", str_length)
/*Use rune to fetchs characters in an array*/
str_char := []rune(str)
fmt.Printf("\n\nCharacter    array:    \n    %c    \n",
str_char)
    for i:= 0 ; i < str_length ; i++ {
        fmt.Printf("\nCharacter at index %d ==> %c\n",
i, str_char[i])
    }
}
```

Output:

14.5 Case conversion

A string can be converted to upper and lower case using the functions **ToUpper** and **ToLower** respectively. Syntax:

<ustring> = strings.ToUpper(<string>)

<lstring> = strings.ToLower(<string>)

Example:

str1 = strings.ToUpper(s)

str2 = strings.ToLower(s)

Here is a program that demonstrates case conversion:

```go
/*Case conversion demo*/
/*Package Declaration*/
package main
/*Import Statement - import fmt, bufio, os, strings
package*/
import (
    "fmt"
    "bufio"
    "os"
    "strings"
    )
/*Mandatory main function*/
func main () {
    /*Create an input reader variable of type NewReader
using stdin*/
    inputReader := bufio.NewReader(os.Stdin)
    /*Prompt the user to enter something*/
    fmt.Printf("\nEnter a string: ")
    /*Read string using ReadString function*/
    str, _ := inputReader.ReadString('\n')
    /*Trim to remove unwanted characters*/
    str = strings.Trim(str, "\n\r")
    /*Convert to upper and lower case*/
    u_str := strings.ToUpper(str)
    l_str := strings.ToLower(str)
    fmt.Printf("\nOriginal   string:   %s\nUpper   case
string: %s\nLower  case  string: %s\n", str, u_str,
l_str)
    }
```

Output:

```
F:\golang>go build caseconversion.go

F:\golang>caseconversion.exe

Enter a string: This is a Case Conversion Demo

Original string: This is a Case Conversion Demo
Upper case string: THIS IS A CASE CONVERSION DEMO
Lower case string: this is a case conversion demo

F:\golang>
```

15. Pointers

When a variable is declared, it is allotted some memory region to store its content. This memory region has a uniquely identifiable address. **Pointers** are special kind of variables that are used to store **addresses of other variables**. An important thing to note here is that a pointer can store the memory address of a variable of the same data type. For example, an integer pointer will store the memory address of an integer variable; a string pointer cannot store the memory address of a floating point variable. A pointer variable is declared using the following syntax:

*var <pointer variable> *<data type>*
Examples:
/ *Integer pointer*/
var ptr *int
/ *String pointers*/
var sptr1, sptr2 *string
/ *Floating point pointer*/
var p *float64

The memory address of a variable can be fetched by prefixing **ampersand (&) symbol** to it. This address can be assigned only to pointer variables of the same data type. Here is how you would do it:

var name string = "Jason"
var sptr *string
sptr = &name
/ *Short declare a pointer*/

var address string = "NY"

add_ptr := &address

/*Declare and initialize pointers*/

var a, b int

var aptr, bptr *int = &a, &b

When a pointer is holding the address of a variable, it is said that the pointer variable is *"pointing to"* that variable. Let us write a program to create a few variables and create the appropriate number of pointers pointing to these variables:

```
/*Pointers Demo 1*/
/*Package Declaration*/
package main
/*Import Statement - import fmt package*/
import ("fmt")
/*Mandatory main function*/
func main () {
 /*Declare and initialize a string*/
 var name string = "Shaun"
 /*Declare a string pointer*/
 var name_ptr *string
 /*Assign the address of name to name_ptr*/
 name_ptr = &name
 /*Short declare and initialize int variable*/
 age := 19
 /*Short declare and initialize integer pointer*/
 aptr := &age
 /*Declare and initialize float variables*/
 var height, weight float32 = 182.36534, 165.75124
 /*Declare and initialize pointer variables pointer
variables*/
 var hptr, wptr *float32 = &height, &weight
 /*Print everything*/
 fmt.Printf("\nname = %s\nname_ptr (address of name
var) = %v\n", name, name_ptr)
 fmt.Printf("\nage = %d\natpr (address of age var) =
%v\n", age, aptr)
 fmt.Printf("\nheight = %f\nhtpr (address of height
var) = %v\n", height, hptr)
```

```
    fmt.Printf("\nweight = %f\nwtpr (address of weight
var) = %v\n", weight, wptr)
    }
```

Output:

In this program, we have just displayed the contents of the variables and their memory addresses. It probably does not make sense to you at this point. You could be asking – what am I suppose to do with the memory address of a variable? Well, we are coming to that. We can **dereference** pointers to directly access the value stored at a memory address that the pointer is pointing to. In order to dereference a pointer, **asterisk (*) symbol** must be prefixed to the pointer variable. Here is a code snippet that explains this concept:

var x int = 90

*var ptr *int = &x*

/*Dereference ptr to access the value of x and assign it to y*/

y := *ptr

The working of this snippet is explained in the following diagram:

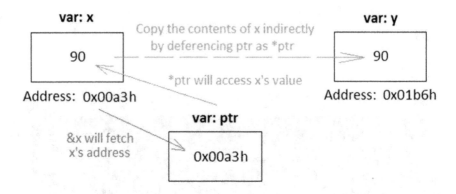

There is an integer variable **x**, initialized to *90*. Let us say, that this variable is stored at memory address *0x00a3h*. An integer pointer variable **ptr** is declared and the address of **x** is assigned to it using the statement **var ptr *int = &x**. Now, **ptr** holds *0x00a3h*. Next, we dereference **ptr** to access the value present at the memory address *0x00a3h (90)* and copy it to another variable **y** (lets say y is at address *0x01b6h*, but that is of no significance in this example). Dereferencing and copying is done using the statement **y := *ptr**. In this example, we managed to copy the contents of one variable to another variable without touching the source variable. Let us understand this concept with the help of a Go program:

```
/*Pointers Demo 2*/
/*Package Declaration*/
package main
/*Import Statement - import fmt package*/
import ("fmt")
/*Mandatory main function*/
func main () {
 /*Declare and initialize a string*/
 var name string = "Anabelle"
 /*Declare a string pointer*/
 var name_ptr *string
 /*Assign the address of name to name_ptr*/
 name_ptr = &name
 /*Short declare and initialize int variable*/
```

```
    age := 33
    /*Short declare and initialize integer pointer*/
    aptr := &age
    /*Print everything*/
    fmt.Printf("\nname = %s\nname_ptr = %v\n*name_ptr =
%s\n", name, name_ptr, *name_ptr)
    fmt.Printf("\nage = %d\natpr = %v\n*aptr = %d\n",
age, aptr, *aptr)
    /*Modify values of name and age without touching
name and age*/
    *name_ptr = "Diorah"
    *aptr = 21
    fmt.Printf("\nname = %s\nname_ptr = %v\n*name_ptr =
%s\n", name, name_ptr, *name_ptr)
    fmt.Printf("\nage = %d\natpr = %v\n*aptr = %d\n",
age, aptr, *aptr)
    }
```

Output:

As seen, there are two variables **name** and **age** which hold some arbitrary initial values. We change the contents of these variables by dereferencing pointers (**name_ptr** and **aptr**) which point to these variables.

If you have understood the concept of variables and pointers well, you may be wondering – a pointer is just another variable and it will have its own address. Yes, a pointer variable has its own address. You can have a pointer which is pointing to another pointer variable. In order to to that, the pointer which is pointing to another pointer will have to be declared as **<data type>. Consider the following code snippet:

```
var x int = 1050
var x_ptr *int = &x
var x_ptr_ptr **int = &xptr
**x_ptr_ptr = 7000
fmt.Println(x)
```

There is an integer variable **x** which holds **1050**. A pointer variable **x_ptr** is used to hold the address of **x** and another pointer variable **x_ptr_ptr** is used to hold the value of **x_ptr**. Single dereferencing of **xptr_ptr** as ***x_ptr_ptr** will give us the value of **x_ptr** which would be the address of **x**. Double dereferencing of **x_ptr_ptr** as ****x_ptr_ptr** will give us the value of **x**. The statement ****x_ptr_ptr = 7000** will change the value of **x** to **7000**.

Note: Pointers is an advanced topic heavily used in data structures, system level programming, embedded systems, etc. If this chapter confuses you, it is quite okay. You can go through the rest of the **book** without any issues. As a beginner, you just have to know what is a pointer and what does it do.

16. Structures

A structure is a user defined data type used to store a collection of elements. Unlike arrays, elements can be of any data type. Structure elements are also called fields. The following syntax is used to define a structure:

type <structure name> struct {
    <field 1> <data type of field 1>
    <field 2> <data type of field 2>
    <field 3> <data type of field 3>
    ...
    <field n> <data type of field n>
}

Let us define a structure to store the details of a ***student*** such as ***student_id, first_name, last_name, age, gpa***:

type student struct {
    student_id int
    first_name string
    last_name string
    gpa float32
}

A structure definition is merely a blueprint of a user defined data type. It does not contain data on its own. In order to make use of a structure definition, variables of that structure type should be created and their fields must be set. Here is how you would create a structure variable:

var <structure variable> <structure name>

Example:

var s1 student

var x, y, student

The fields of a structure variable can be set as follows:

<structure variable>.<field> = <value>

Example:

var s student

s.student_id = 100014

s.first_name = "Grant"

s.last_name = "Dewan"

s.age = 16

Here is an example that defines a structure, create a structure variable, sets its fields and prints them on the console:

```
/*Structures Demo 1*/
/*Package Declaration*/
package main
/*Import Statement - import fmt package*/
import ("fmt")
/*Define a structure*/
/*Set 3 fields*/
type student struct {
 s_id int
 f_name string
 l_name string
 grade int
 age int
 gpa float32
}
/*Mandatory main function*/
func main () {
 /*Declare a structure variable S of type student*/
 var S student
 /*Set fields of S*/
 S.s_id = 30657095
```

```
S.f_name = "Sophia"
S.l_name = "Johnson"
S.grade = 12
S.age = 18
S.gpa = 8.97
/*Print S' details*/
fmt.Printf("\nStudent - S\n")
fmt.Printf("\nS.s_id = %d", S.s_id)
fmt.Printf("\nS.f_name = %s", S.f_name)
fmt.Printf("\nS.l_name = %s", S.l_name)
fmt.Printf("\nS.grade = %d", S.grade)
fmt.Printf("\nS.age = %d", S.age)
/*Print gpa, restrict to 2 decimal places*/
fmt.Printf("\nS.gpa = %.2f\n", S.gpa)
}
```

Output:

A structure variable can also be initialized using the following syntax:

var <struct var> <struct name> = <struct name>{<field 1>:<value 1>, ..., <field n>:<value n>}

Example:

var s1 student = student {student_id: 231, first_name: "Rajat", last_name: "Singh", age: 20}

Short-declaring a structure variable is also possible with the following syntax:

<struct var> := = <struct name>{<field 1>:<value 1>, ..., <field n>:<value n>}

Example:

s2 := student {student_id: 592, first_name: "Jorge", last_name: "Fernandez", age: 17}

Here is a program that shows all the methods of field setting:

```
/*Structures Demo 2*/
/*Package Declaration*/
package main
/*Import Statement - import fmt package*/
import ("fmt")
/*Define a structure*/
/*Set 3 fields*/
type person struct {
 name string
 address string
 age int
}
/*Mandatory main function*/
func main () {
 /*Declare a structure variable p1*/
 var p1 person
 /*Set fields of p1*/
 p1.name = "Earl"
 p1.address = "NJ"
 p1.age = 25
 /*Declare and initialize a structure variable p2*/
 var p2 person = person {name: "Manjunath", address:
"New Delhi", age: 30}
 /*Short declare and initialize structure variable
p3*/
 p3 := person {name: "Bella", address: "London",
age: 19}
 fmt.Printf("\nperson p1\n")
 fmt.Printf("\np1.name = %s\np1.address = %s\np1.age
= %d\n", p1.name, p1.address, p1.age)
 fmt.Printf("\nperson p2\n")
 fmt.Printf("\np2.name = %s\np2.address = %s\np2.age
= %d\n", p2.name, p2.address, p2.age)
 fmt.Printf("\nperson p3\n")
```

```
    fmt.Printf("\np3.name = %s\np3.address = %s\np3.age
= %d\n", p3.name, p3.address, p3.age)
    }
```

Output:

17. Programming Examples

Now that we have gone through the basics of Go programming, let us put those concepts to use and try out some programming examples.

17.1 Sum of digits of a number

Here is a program that reads an integer from the user and calculates the sum of its digits:

```go
/*Sum of digits*/
/*Package Declaration*/
package main
/*Import Statement - import fmt package*/
import ("fmt")
/*Mandatory main function*/
func main () {
 var number int
 var sum int = 0
 fmt.Printf("\nEnter a number: ")
 fmt.Scanf("%d", &number)
 for number > 0 {
     /*Add one's digit to sum*/
     sum = sum + ( number % 10 ) ;
     /*Discard one's digit*/
     number = number / 10 ;
 }
 fmt.Printf("\nSum of all digits: %d\n", sum)
 }
```

Output:

```
F:\golang>go build sumofdigits.go
F:\golang>sumofdigits.exe
Enter a number: 4970256
Sum of all digits: 33
F:\golang>
```

17.2 Fibonacci series

Fibonacci series begins with the terms 0 and 1. The next term is derived by adding the previous two terms. Since first two terms are 0 and 1, the next terms will be 1, 2, 3, 5, 8 and so son. Here is the program:

```go
/*Fibonacci Series*/
/*Package Declaration*/
package main
/*Import Statement - import fmt package*/
import ("fmt")
/*Mandatory main function*/
func main () {
 var terms, next int
 var previous, current int = 0, 1
 fmt.Printf("\nEnter the number of terms to be generated: ")
 fmt.Scanf("%d", &terms)
 if (terms < 2) {
     fmt.Printf("\nFibonacci series contains at least two terms")
 } else {
     fmt.Printf("\n\nFibonacci series:\n\n")
     for i := 0 ; i < ( terms ) ; i ++ {
         fmt.Printf("%d ", previous)
         next = previous + current
         previous = current
         current = next
     }
 }
 fmt.Printf("\n")
 }
```

<u>Output:</u>

```
F:\golang>fibo
Enter the number of terms to be generated: 20

Fibonacci series:

0 1 1 2 3 5 8 13 21 34 55 89 144 233 377 610 987 1597 2584 4181
F:\golang>
```

17.3 Reverse a given number

Here is a program that reads an integer and reverses it:

```
/*Reverse a number*/
/*Package Declaration*/
package main
/*Import Statement - import fmt package*/
import ("fmt")
/*Mandatory main function*/
func main () {
 var number int
 var rev int = 0
 fmt.Printf("\nEnter a number: ")
 fmt.Scanf("%d", &number)
 for ( number > 0 ) {
     rev = (rev * 10 ) + ( number % 10 )
     number = number / 10
 }
 fmt.Printf("\nReverse: %d\n", rev)
 }
```

Output:

```
Command Prompt                                    _ □ ×
F:\golang>go build revdigits.go
F:\golang>revdigits.exe
Enter a number: 123456789
Reverse: 987654321
F:\golang>_
```

17.4 String Palindrome

A string is said to be a palindrome if its reverse is the same as the original string. For example, the word "book" is not a palindrome while the word "malayalam" is a palindrome. Following is a program that receives a string as an input and checks if it is a palindrome. Note that case-sensitivity is not accounted for.

```go
/*Palindrome*/
/*Package Declaration*/
package main
/*Import Statement - import fmt, bufio, os, strings
package*/
import (
    "fmt"
    "bufio"
    "os"
    "strings"
    )
/*Mandatory main function*/
func main () {
/*Create an input reader variable of type NewReader
using stdin*/
    inputReader := bufio.NewReader(os.Stdin)
    /*Prompt the user to enter something*/
    fmt.Printf("\nEnter a string: ")
    /*Read string using ReadString function*/
    str, _ := inputReader.ReadString('\n')
    /*Trim \n and \r characters*/
    str = strings.Trim(str, "\n\r")
    str_length := len(str) - 1
    /*Use rune to fetchs characters in an array*/
    str_char := []rune(str)
    /*Reverse str*/
    for i := 0 ; i < str_length/2 ; i++ {
        temp := str_char[i]
        str_char[i] = str_char[str_length-i]
        str_char[str_length-i] = temp
    }
    /*Convert back to string using string function*/
    rev_str := string(str_char)
    fmt.Printf("\nReversed string: %s\n", rev_str)
    /*Check if both strings are equal*/
    result := strings.Compare(str, rev_str)
    if (result == 0) {
        fmt.Printf("\n%s is a palindrome.\n", str)
    } else {
        fmt.Printf("\n%s is not a palindrome.\n", str)
    }
}
```

Output:

```
F:\golang>go build strpal.go
F:\golang>strpal.exe
Enter a string: positive world
Reversed string: dlrow evitisop
positive world is not a palindrome.
F:\golang>strpal.exe
Enter a string: madam
Reversed string: madam
madam is a palindrome.
F:\golang>
```

17.5 Bubble Sort

Bubble sort is an algorithm for sorting data structures in ascending or descending order. In this algorithm, two loops are used in a nested manner. The inner loop makes sure that the greatest or the smallest element is either placed at the beginning or the end of the data structure. The number of iterations that the outer loop goes through is equal to the number of elements in the data structure. We will write a program to read 5 integers from the user, put them in an array and sort the array in ascending order using bubble sort.

```go
/*Sorting array using Bubble Sort*/
/*Package Declaration*/
package main
/*Import Statement - import fmt package*/
import (
    "fmt"
    "strconv"
    )
/*Mandatory main function*/
func main () {
 /*Declare variables*/
 var arr [5] int
 /*Declare two loop counters*/
 var i, j int
```

145

```go
    /*Declare a variable to temporarily store num as
string*/
    var num_str string
    /*Prompt the user to enter 5 elements, use for
loop*/
    for i = 0 ; i < 5 ; i++ {
        fmt.Printf("\nEnter element at index %d: ", i)
        fmt.Scanln(&num_str)
        /*Convert num_str to integer*/
        num, err := strconv.Atoi(num_str)
        /*Assign num to arr[i]*/
        arr[i] = num
        /*Assign err to blank identifier*/
        _ = err
    }
    fmt.Printf("\nOriginal array: %d\n", arr)
    arr_length := len(arr)
    /*Bubble sort*/
    for i = 0 ; i < arr_length ; i++ {
        for j = 0 ; j < i ; j++ {
            if (arr[j] > arr[j + 1]) {
                temp := arr[j]
                arr[j] = arr[j + 1]
                arr[j + 1] = temp
            }
        }
    }
    fmt.Printf("\nSorted array: %d\n", arr)
}
```

Output:

18. Final Words

Go programming language is a relatively new one. The first version was released in 2012, so at the time of writing this book, it is just about 8 years old in 2020. This language has great potential with the kind of features that it offers. My aim behind writing this book was to get my readers acquainted with a new programming language which could revolutionize software development in the near future. I have tried my best to keep concepts in the book very simple so that your basics become very clear.

Go language is already turning out to be a game changer when it comes to web development, cloud application development, middleware development, etc. If you have already understood the basic concepts explained in this book, you should definitely learn more and perhaps get your hands on some of the advanced concepts such as object oriented programming, file handling, error handling, etc. If you are a web developer already, you should try web frameworks such as *Gin, Web.Go, Martini, Revel*, etc. to develop web applications and services.

Hope you have learned something of value from this book.

Always remember – Learning never ends!

If you enjoyed this book as much as I've enjoyed writing it, you can subscribe* to my email list for exclusive content and sneak peaks of my future books.

Visit the link below:

http://eepurl.com/du_L4n

OR

Use the QR Code:

(*Must be 13 years or older to subscribe)

www.ingramcontent.com/pod-product-compliance
Lightning Source LLC
LaVergne TN
LVHW051342050326
832903LV00031B/3697